GERMAN JETS
VERSUS
THE U.S.
ARMY
AIR FORCE

WILLIAM N. HESS
OFFICIAL HISTORIAN FOR THE AMERICAN FIGHTER ACES ASSOCIATION

© 1996 William N. Hess

Edited by Lisa Hanks

Published by:
Specialty Press Publishers and Wholesalers
11481 Kost Dam Road
North Branch, MN 55056
612/583-3239

Printed in the United States of America

Designed by Greg Compton

ISBN
0-933424-63-9

TABLE OF CONTENTS

THE VIEW FROM THE COCKPIT

I t has been my desire to do this book ever since my research began while delving into the official records of U.S. Army Air Force units at Maxwell Air Force Base, Alabama, in the early 1960s. Kenn Rust and I teamed up to do an article entitled "The German Jets and the U.S. Army Air Force" for *The American Aviation Historical Society Journal*, Fall 1963, issue.

Over the years, I kept digging up bits of material while researching for books that I have done. Then, when I was able to acquire copies of nearly all 8th Fighter Command Pilots Encounters Reports in recent years, I was able to complete more than ninety percent of the story from the fighter pilot's viewpoint. (The view from the bomber

The Me 262 was the most revolutionary and best-performing fighter produced during World War II. Its jet engines and heavy armament presented a dangerous challenge to all Allied aircraft. (via Ethell)

crew's perspective has already been obtained during a number of projects in that field.)

This is the story of the combats that took place from late summer of 1944 up until the end of the war in Europe in May of 1945. It depicts a campaign that began when the Messerschmitt 163 and Messerschmitt 262 made their first appearances and struck fear into the heart of the leaders of the Eighth Air Force and particularly those in 8th Bomber Command. It suddenly made the outstanding performance of the North American P-51 Mustangs obsolete. Therein began an investigation into tactics to protect the bombers and a fervent hope that the new enemy fighters would not become available in great numbers. The final tactics plus the triumphs and tragedies for both sides are told in these pages.

Following the Battle of the Bulge during December 1944, the American press seemingly took the attitude that the war in Europe was over and very little publicity was given to the continuing air war over Europe despite the fact that Allied fighter forces continued to battle the new Luftwaffe jets and that bomber crews were still attacking in force while sustaining heavy losses, some of which were due to the appearance of the new German aircraft. Even after World War II, there was so little publicity concerning the German jets that the popular view was that perhaps only a dozen jets, if that many, had ever been downed by fighter pilots of the U.S. Army Air Forces. If the jets downed any Allied bombers, no one seemed to know anything about it.

I have done my best to include details of all the combats, during which the fighter pilots of the U.S. Army Air Forces received credit for 165 Luftwaffe jets. As best I could, I have included the highlights from the contests between the aircrews of the American bombers and the German jet pilots. There was great determination and heroism on both sides, and I hope that I have given both some long overdue praise.

WILLIAM N. HESS
1996

GERMAN JETS VS. THE U.S. ARMY AIR FORCE

CHAPTER 1

THE JET MENACE DEFINED

W ithout a doubt, the Messerschmitt 262 was the most revolutionary and extraordinary fighter plane to appear in World War II. It continues to be a controversial aircraft in that there are those who believe it could have changed the complexion of the war over Europe had it appeared in significant numbers earlier and had it been made available strictly as a fighter plane. The legendary edict issued by Adolph Hitler that the Messerschmitt enter the conflict as a bomber is still open to argument, in that its production as a fighter was not as restricted as it has been usually pictured. Basically, the main delays in putting the Messerschmitt 262 into action were numerous delays in supplying the new turbojet engines for the waiting airframes and then keeping the aircraft operating once they were in combat units. Many other delays were due to Allied bombing of the plants that built the aircraft and the engines, fuel shortages, political interference and the inexperience of many of the young pilots who were checked out in the new fighter.

However, when the Me 262 finally flew into action with veteran pilots at its controls, the aircraft struck fear into the hearts of the men in the Allied bombers. The Allies quickly discovered that a solid burst of fire from the Messerschmitt's four 30 MM cannon caused such extensive damage to their aircraft that, if struck, they had little chance of making it home again. The Allied fighter pilots were intensely aware of the fighter's superiority: the jet could outdistance them with ease and one burst of fire striking their aircraft spelt certain destruction. Yet, they accepted the challenge for they had their ability and superiority in numbers, they had discovered a key vulnerability of the Me 262 in dogfighting, and above all, they knew they could destroy the jet while it was taking off and landing.

The original concept for the Messerschmitt 262 originated in 1938 when the German Reich Ministry issued a request for an airframe design to house two turbojet engines that were being developed by

BMW. The BMW designers estimated that the new engines would develop a nominal thrust of 1,320 pounds and would be available for an airframe by December 1939.

The airframe design study was taken up by a Messerschmitt team headed by Woldenmar Voigt. The original design called for an all-metal, low-winged monoplane with a retractable landing gear and two turbojet engines housed in the wing roots. The wingspan and length were both a few inches longer than thirty feet and, by calculating the design to the thrust, the estimated maximum speed of the aircraft was to be an astounding 560 miles per hour.

On the strength of that outstanding calculation, Messerschmitt was commissioned to prepare a mockup of the design, which was designated Project 1065. The ministry examined the mockup on

Early on, the only training for Me 262 pilots was by word-of-mouth. Here one Luftwaffe pilot goes over the cockpit controls with a student. (via Ethell)

THE JET MENACE DEFINED

March 1, 1940, and Messerschmitt was ordered to construct three prototypes under the leadership of Rudolf Seitz.

During the construction of the prototypes, the team discovered that the BMW engines had failed to live up to expectations and would be unable to power the airframes. However, Junkers was in the process of developing the Jumo 004 engine, created by Dr. Anselm Franz. This engine was first run in November 1940, but it immediately encountered difficulties.

As a stopgap measure, a Junkers Jumo 12-cylinder liquid-cooled engine was fitted to the aircraft in order to permit airframe testing. The aircraft was airborne under the guidance of test pilot Fritz Wendel on April 18, 1941, and despite some difficulty in coaxing the overweight aircraft into the air, the performance of the airframe was very favorable. The prototype, designated V1, would take to the air a number of times over the next few months, but during one of its more significant flights, the piston-powered Jumo engine was supplemented by experimental BMW turbojets. Wendel, once again, took off in the aircraft to test the turbojets, only to have one, and then the other, flame out. Only with great difficulty was Wendel able to safely land the aircraft back on the ground.

Junkers continued to work on their 004 turbojet engine, and in time, two of the engines were delivered to Leipheim, where they were fitted to the Messerschmitt Me 262 V3 for testing. On the morning of July 18, 1942, Wendel did some taxi testing and then roared down the runway for the initial takeoff. Unfortunately, he was unable to get any response from the elevator and thus could not get airborne. The ground crew suggested that when the aircraft reached 112 MPH, Wendel could touch the brakes and the "kick" would be enough to raise the tail and give him some elevator control. Wendel tapped the brakes, and sure enough, it was successful. This was the first jet flight of the Me 262. All in all, the flight went well, and the development team was enthused by its result. Their next major modification involved extending the leading edge slots completely across the entire center section of the wing.

The Me 262 V3 made six further test flights before it was involved in an accident with air ministry test pilot, Beauvais, at the controls. The accident delayed testing somewhat and it was October 1, 1942, before Me 262 V2 made its initial flight. The success of this aircraft was rewarded when the existing order for fifteen pre-production aircraft was doubled, making a total of forty-five machines on order.

As the new and improved Jumo 004 engines were produced, the Me 262 was tested further and more intensively. The primary difficulty with the aircraft at this time was the continued failure of the turbine blades. Nickel and chrome were in short supply in Germany and it would be months before the Junkers engineers would be able to develop new, hollow blades that, once installed, added immensely to the aircraft's performance and reliability.

The other major change that took place in the development of the Me 262 was the installation of landing gear rather than the old conventional "tail dragger" configuration. One of the primary promoters of this change was General of the Fighters Adolf Galland, who made his first flight in the Me 262 in April. Galland was so impressed by the aircraft that he wanted all production of the Messerschmitt 109 halted and fighter production restricted to the Messerschmitt 262 and the Focke Wulf 190.

Leutenantgeneral Adolf Galland flew the Me 262 in April of 1943, and, recognizing its enormous potential, wanted the aircraft put into production immediately. Galland championed the aircraft up until the end of the war, when he led a select squadron of Me 262 pilots from the JV 44 unit.

THE JET MENACE DEFINED

Galland's request did not come to pass, but the Me 262 was ordered into production in June 1943. Many delays occurred, and one of the biggest was due to the American bombing raid on Regensburg on August 17, 1943, which destroyed a large number of the production jigs. Immediately after, the Germans began to disperse production parts, and as time went on, an excellent network was set up whereby production of the Me 262 suffered little from further Allied bombing attacks.

At the beginning of November 1943, the first preproduction model of the Me 262 joined the flight test program. This model was fitted with new Jumo 004-B1 engines, which produced 1,980

A series of excellent photos shows an early production version of the Me 262. The aircraft had a top speed of 536 MPH, which enabled it to speed away from the P-51 Mustangs that escorted the targeted bombers. The 30 MM cannon, located in its nose, struck fear in the hearts of the bomber crews. The banking aircraft shows the aircraft's fine lines, but its unexceptional turn performance eventually became its downfall when the Me 262 engaged in combat with the piston-driven Allied fighters. (via Ethell)

THE JET MENACE DEFINED

pounds of thrust. No armament was fitted, but the aircraft possessed the new tricycle landing gear. On November 26, the Me 262 was demonstrated for Hitler, and this is when the story regarding the Me 262's use as a bomber was established. Hitler asked if the aircraft could carry bombs and he was told that it could. He then declared that the Me 262 was to become a "blitz-bomber." However, documentation that came to light following the war indicated what Hitler really meant was that the Me 262 would become a fighter-bomber.

In December 1943, two further preproduction Me 262 models became available; one of them served as a test aircraft for the armament system of the new jet. Four 30 MM Rheinmetall-Borsig MK 108 cannon with electropneumatic cocking and electrical firing were installed, which were to be used in conjunction with a Revi 16B sight. Some initial difficulties arose, but these were solved by a rerouting of the ammunition belts. The two upper guns were provided with 100 rounds per gun, and the two lower guns with eighty rounds.

In January and February 1944, the remaining twenty-three preproduction Me 262 airframes became available, but they could not be finished due to the lack of turbojet engines. The Jumo 004-B1 was currently being installed not only in the Me 262, but also in the new Arado 234, which delayed the combat-readiness of both types of aircraft.

The first production Me 262A-1a Schwalbe (Swallow) came off the line armed with four MK 108 cannon, and this fighter model possessed an impressive combat capability. The Swallow's maximum level speed was at 22,880 feet, where it reached 536 miles per hour. Its rate of climb was 1,937 feet per minute, and its critical Mach number was .86 in a dive. One of its drawbacks was a tendency to flame out at high speeds and at altitudes above 26,000 feet, but if flown by an experienced pilot, the aircraft would climb to 41,000 feet.

The production of the bomber version of the aircraft was designated Me 262A-2a and called the Sturmvogel (Stormbird). The Sturmvogel carried two 30 MM MK 108 cannon, and it was capable of carrying one 2,205-pound (1,000-kilogram), two 1,100-pound (500-kilogram) or two 550-pound (250-kilogram) bombs. Bombing was to take place from a thirty-degree dive at a speed of 530 to 550 miles per hour, which was obtained before the pilot pulled out at 3,000 to 3,500 feet.

The first operational sorties were flown by the Erprobungskommando unit, which was based at Lechfeld in April 1944. It was staffed by a nucleus of Messerschmitt test pilots, who continued to put the aircraft through all possible scenarios to check out its capability. These pilots also trained the Luftwaffe pilots who were to fly the Me 262 into combat. The unit, under the command of Hauptmann Thierfelder, did fly some combat sorties, primarily against Royal Air Force reconnaissance aircraft.

An early production model of the Me 262 fighter-bomber version is being loaded with bombs. The aircraft was capable of carrying more than one ton of bombs. (via Ethell)

THE JET MENACE DEFINED

The first fighter-bomber unit was a detachment of KG 51, commanded by Major Wolfgang Schenck, whose Kommando unit flew its first sorties over northern France in August 1944.

Although 1,430 Me 262s were built, most of them never saw combat, and many were still missing vital parts when the war ended. Fuel and parts shortages so affected the operational units that they could rarely get half their aircraft flying. On any given day, up until the end of the war in Europe, the Luftwaffe could get no more than fifty to sixty Me 262s airborne at one time.

THE MESSERSCHMITT 163—THE KOMET

The rocket-powered Messerschmitt 163 Komet owed its existence to Dr. Alexander Lippish, who had begun to design tailless gliders in 1926. The craft proved to be so successful and possessed such excel-

The exotic Me 163 gets its engines started. Its rocket-engine fuel was so volatile that starting the engines was the most dangerous step in its flight procedure. (via Ethell)

lent handling characteristics that it was fitted with an eight-horse-power engine and made its first powered flight in September 1929.

Over the years, Lippish had designed several successful tailless gliders, a few of which featured a delta wing design. In 1939, Lippish was asked by the German Air Ministry to come up with a design to utilize a new, secret rocket engine, the Walter I-203, which produced 882 pounds of thrust. The engine was powered by two fuels that reacted violently to each other: *T-stoff*, which consisted mainly of concentrated hydrogen peroxide; and *Z-stoff*, a solution of calcium permanganate in water. Due to the forceful reaction of the propellants, it was necessary to construct the fuselage of metal, which meant that Lippish and his staff must work with the Heinkel facility.

However, the new rocket-propelled plane never developed as it had been hoped, and Heinkel never did build the metal fuselage. It was finally decided that Lippish and his design staff would join the Messerschmitt firm at Augsburg, although Messerschmitt was not enthused with Lippish's project. In early 1940, instead of a metal fuselage, Lippish fitted an all-wood airframe design, called DFS 194, with the Walter RI-203 engine at Peenemunde-West. On June 3, 1940, test pilot Heini Dittmar took the aircraft on its maiden flight and successfully reached a speed of 340 miles per hour in level flight.

Following this success, Lippish was instructed to design an aircraft that would use the latest rocket engine, the Walter II-203b, which was rated at 1,653 pounds of thrust. The design was to be a high-speed, fast-climbing interceptor that could stay on the ground until the enemy was almost overhead. With this strategy, the brief endurance of the rocket-powered flight would not be a negative factor. Thus was born the Messerschmitt 163.

The new design made its first unpowered flights in the spring of 1941, when it was towed aloft by Messerschmitt 110s. The design's flying characteristics were very good, and it was sent to Peenemunde-West in the summer of 1941, where it was fitted with the new Walter engine. The performance of this aircraft in the air was outstanding, and with Dittmar once more in the pilot's seat, it reached a speed of 550 miles per hour. However, on the ground a number of unfortunate experiences occurred with the Me 163. Z-stoff began to clog the engine jets, which resulted in violent explosions. A number of people were killed testing the engines, and one entire building was destroyed.

The first of the new Me 163 prototypes became available in April 1942. The troublesome Z-stoff had been replaced by *C-stoff*, which was a hydrazine hydrate solution in methyl alcohol. The design featured a sweepback of the wing's leading edge, the metal fuselage was larger with an enlarged pilot's compartment and ventral housing for the hydraulically operated landing skid. The jettisonable wheel feature was retained, and more space was provided for radio, armor and the propellant fuels.

In August 1942, Dittmar suffered severe injuries during a rough landing, and he had to be replaced by Hauptman Wolfgang Spate and Rudolph Opitz. Testing continued and the design team installed a new engine, the Walter 109-509A-2, which produced 3,470 pounds of thrust. In early 1943, a new phase of training for the Me 163 was entered, and a new training unit, designated Erlprobungskommando 16, was established at Peenemunde-West. At this time, two 20 MM cannon were also installed in the Me 163.

Despite the bombing of Peenemunde, the unit continued to train there. However, soon thereafter the unit, with a strength of some thirty pilots, was moved to Bad Zwischenahn. Pilots began their training for the Me 163 flying in gliders, then advanced to being towed aloft for unpowered flights in the Me 163. Training during powered flights was dangerous due to the explosive power of the fuels and the fact that landings permitted no second chances, even though the aircraft came in at 137 MPH.

While pilots trained, building of the Me 163 production models was delayed by the bombing of the Messerschmitt plant at Regensburg on August 17, 1943. Following this attack, the aircraft manufacturing process was broken up into its major component parts, which were split up for manufacture at various points around Germany. And as things really began to form, Wolfgang Spate, the key man in the program, was transferred to the Eastern Front. Spate had hoped to initiate the formation of a number of Me 163 bases dotted across Germany, all set within 93 miles of each other, which would enable the aircraft to return to bases easily following combat. Spate had also come close to scoring the first Me 163 victory when he lined up on an American P-47 Thunderbolt, but as he increased his speed for the kill, he went into compressibility.

The production Me 163Bs were equipped with two 30 MM cannon mounted in the wing roots, each with boxes for 120 rounds of

Rudolf "Pitz" Opitz climbs up toward the cockpit of an Me 163. Opitz was the primary test pilot on the aircraft. Note the propeller on the nose, which ran a generator that provided the electrical power during flight. (via Ethell)

THE JET MENACE DEFINED

ammunition. The aircraft featured a Revi 16B gunsight, a 90 MM armored glass screen beneath the Plexiglas canopy and armor behind the pilot's back and over the nose cone. When faced with combat, the pilot had to immediately climb to reach interception altitude; the total engine time at full throttle was only seven and one-half minutes. In most cases, the pilot had to throttle back to get any kind of attack on a bomber, which made him susceptible to fire from the gunners. If hit, bail outs at high-speed were impossible, and hits on the aircraft's fuel system could easily provoke a violent explosion.

The Me 163 became operational with the JG 400 unit at Brandis, where its mission was to defend the Leuna oil refineries. The first major engagement came on August 16, 1944, when five Me 163s rose to intercept B-17s that were attacking the oil refineries. The Me 163s scored hits on one Flying Fortress, but the Komets took two losses.

The Arado 234 was a sleek and modern jet aircraft that the Germans used mostly as a bomber, but as a high-speed, high-altitude reconnaissance plane, it was unsurpassed. (via Ethell)

Nearly 300 Me 163s were in front line service at the end of the war, but only nine victories were gained by the aircraft. Although casualties were high in Me 163 units, only fourteen of the aircraft were lost in combat. A full eighty percent of their losses came during landings and takeoffs. Truly, the Me 163 was an exceptional aircraft many years ahead of its time in many of its features. Perhaps it was a much better psychological weapon than it was an interceptor.

ARADO 234

The concept for the Arado 234 sprouted in 1940 when engineers began work on a reconnaissance-type aircraft to be powered by a new turbojet engine that was being developed by either BMW or by Junkers. By the spring of 1941, a design had been completed for a conventional shoulder-wing monoplane that incorporated a very slim fuselage. The pilot was to be encased in a rounded Plexiglas nose compartment, which would be pressurized for high-altitude operations. The most unusual feature of the aircraft's design was its undercarriage. Rather than conventional landing gear, the plane would use a jettisonable three-wheel trolley, which would be released and parachuted back to earth once the craft was airborne. When it came time to land, the Arado 234 would come in on three skids— glider fashion.

Two prototypes were completed in the winter of 1941 and 1942, but it was not until February 1943 that the first two Junkers 00B-0 turbojets became available. Taxi tests began in March, and finally, the aircraft was transferred to Rheine airdrome, where it was fitted with two new jet engines. On June 15, 1943, the Arado 234 was piloted on its maiden flight by test pilot Flugkaptan Selle. The flight went well, but the trolley used for takeoff was destroyed when the parachutes failed to open after its release at 2,000 feet.

A successful second flight took place on August 10, but once more the parachutes on the trolley failed to deploy. Nine days later, the third test flight took place and this time the trolley was jettisoned soon after the aircraft became airborne. However, the pilot experienced difficulties with the aircraft and was forced to crash land. The plane never flew again.

The test program suffered a setback on October 1, 1943, when during a test flight of the other prototype, Selle reported a fire in the aircraft's port engine. As he descended, flames were seen streaming back. The pilot bailed out, but he was too low for his parachute to open.

The design team decided to fit the Arado 234 with a landing gear. The trolley and skids worked during later test flights, but getting the aircraft back on the trolley following landing took too much time; in a combat zone the inability to move the plane quickly could spell disaster. The team attached two conventional landing gear so they retracted into a widened fuselage and installed a nose gear that retracted below the pilot's position.

The newly modified aircraft was designated Arado 234B, and the first prototype of that model, the AR 234 V9, flew on March 10, 1944. This prototype not only had an undercarriage, but also a new pressurized cabin and a rear-view periscope for the pilot.

The success of this new design quickly led to a demand for the aircraft to be place in production. A reconnaissance version of the aircraft, the Arado 234B-1, carried two cameras of various size mounted in the rear of the fuselage. The Arado 234B-2, the bomber version, was capable of carrying a maximum of 3,000 pounds of bombs, one mounted under the fuselage and one under each engine. The bomber version was fitted with a bombing computer that taxed the ability of the pilot—he had to push his control column to the side in order to use the bombsight.

Early in July 1944, two of the early versions of the Arado 234 were delivered to an experimental unit of the Luftwaffe (I/Versuchsverband Ob.d.L.) based at Juvincourt near Rheims, France. From this base, the first reconnaissance mission was flown on August 2, 1944, when Arado 234 V-7 flew over the Allied beachheads of France at 30,000 feet to take pictures of the various sites. The aircraft returned safely and delivered the first really good film that the German high command had been able to obtain since D-Day in France.

In September 1944, this reconnaissance unit, which had been renamed Kommando Sperling, was moved to Rheine in northwest Germany. Here the unit began to receive Arado 234Bs, the production-type aircraft with conventional landing gear. These aircraft usually flew their missions at altitudes higher than 29,000 feet and could cruise at between 435 and 450 MPH, which pretty well freed them from the fear of Allied fighter attacks. Another pleasing feature of the Arado 234 was that the engines gave little trouble, despite the fact that they were only good for only twenty-five to thirty hours.

An early model Arado 234 jettisons the dolly it used for take-off as it becomes airborne. The dolly soon proved intractable and inefficient, so a tricycle landing gear was fitted to the Arado. (via Ethell)

THE JET MENACE DEFINED

In June 1944, the first bomber pilots from the Arado bomber unit, KG 76, arrived at the Arado factory to begin receiving instruction on flying the new planes. A number of the pilots were killed during this training. Eventually, the pilots were allowed to spend flying time in the Messerschmitt 262 jet before switching to the Arado. Their training delayed the operational status of KG 76. They would not fly into action with the Arado jets until December 1944, when the first unit of sixteen aircraft was established at Munster/Handorf.

Bombers from KG 76 were active in the area of Liege during the German offensive in the Ardennes. They continued to try to support Germany ground forces when the Battle of the Bulge ceased and the retreat into Germany began.

In March 1945, quite a few missions were flown by Arado 234s from KG 76 when American forces captured the Ludendorff railroad bridge, which crossed the Rhine River at Remagen. Day after day, the German aircraft attempted to break through the American defenses. Several of the jet bombers were shot down by Allied fighters and ground fire during this period.

By the end of March, the bombing missions for KG 76 in the Arado 234 were almost over. Very few missions were flown near the end of the war.

The last Arado 234 reconnaissance unit formed was Sonderkommando Sommer, which was based at Udine, Italy. This unit utilized three aircraft in high-altitude photo missions that followed the movements of Allied troops.

Although only some 200 Arado 234Bs were built, this aircraft model certainly made its mark in World War II as the first jet twin-engined bomber and the first jet high-altitude reconnaissance aircraft.

CHAPTER 2

ENTER THE JET MENACE

The introduction of the German jets to operational service did not come as a surprise to the Allies. They had known through intelligence service of the jets' existence, and later photographs began to appear that showed the jets on the ground as high-flying photo reconnaissance missions began to pick them out.

Top-secret messages intercepted from German Enigma-coded messages chronicled the establishment and location of new jet units in the Luftwaffe. The Allies knew that it was only a matter of time before these jets would be encountered in the air.

Eprobungskommando 262 (Ekdo 262) was the experimental fighter unit formed around the nucleus of the new Messerschmitt 262. This unit was initially created at Lechfeld in December of 1943, but it did not begin to receive the aircraft in which to train new pilots until April 1944. Due to Hitler's insistence that the jet become a blitz-bomber, the first student pilots assigned to Ekdo 262 came from 3/ZG 26, a Messerschmitt 110 unit.

MAY 1944

The first attack against American aircraft was probably flown in May 1944 by Major Wolfgang Spate, who had trained the 1st Squadron of JG 400 how to fly the rocket-propelled Messerschmitt 163. Spate took off from Bad Zwischenahn on May 13, and soon after was vectored to intercept two American P-47 Thunderbolt fighters. As he closed on them, his rocket engine quit and he had to go through a frustrating restart procedure in order to pick up the chase. Finally, the engine refired and Spate quickly closed the gap.

He found himself close behind the P-47s, whose pilots were obviously never aware that he was there. Just as he flew into firing range, his aircraft's left wing dropped suddenly and Spate began to lose control of his craft. By the time he had regained control and cut his speed, the Thunderbolts were gone. Spate had reached that point of compressibility with his aircraft, its speed had reached its maximum capability. His opportunity for victory had escaped him.

June and July 1944

In June 1944, the first blitz-bomber unit, KG (J) 51 Eidelweiss, began to receive its Me 262s. Its pilots were rapidly checked out in the jet aircraft at Lechfeld, and by July, the 3/JG 51 unit had been moved to Chateaudun near Orleans in France. There, it began bombing operations against Allied forces that had landed in Normandy on June 6, 1944.

The 262 pilots were not allowed to fly their aircraft lower than 13,000 feet for fear that they might be downed by ground fire and fall into the hands of Allied ground forces. They had no means of accurately dropping their bombs, so their operational results were almost nil. As Allied troops broke out and raced swiftly across France, the jets of JG 51 were forced to retreat from one airfield to another. By August 1944, the unit was flying from bases in Belgium.

The first officially recorded meeting between an Allied aircraft and a Luftwaffe jet occurred on July 25, 1944. On that day, a DeHaviland Mosquito from the RAF's No. 544 Squadron, piloted by Flight Lieutenant A.E. Wall with Flight Officer A.S. Lobban on board as observer, was on a photo reconnaissance mission at 29,000 feet when Lobban sighted a twin-engined aircraft closing rapidly from some 400 yards astern.

Once alerted by his observer, Wall gave his Mosquito full throttle and was startled to see his opponent pass him up and pull up to the right and above him. As the Me 262 began to turn to the left, Wall broke right, but the enemy craft was immediately on his tail and closing fast. At about 800 yards, the enemy pilot opened fire, and Wall commenced a gentle, tight turn to the left, which enabled the Mosquito to turn inside the 262. When Wall's aircraft was almost on the tail of the jet, the Luftwaffe pilot broke away.

Three times the enemy pilot repeated his maneuver, and each time Wall was able to break sharply and turn inside the 262. On his final pass the Luftwaffe pilot tried to pull up under the Mosquito, but Wall broke as sharply as possible to the left and up. Two muffled explosions were heard, and Wall, sure they had been hit, told Lobban to open the emergency hatch. When he did so, Lobban discovered that the explosions had been the outer hatch blowing off due to the intensity of their maneuver.

Hall sighted some cumulus clouds below and went after their cover in a dive. When he pulled out of the clouds three or four minutes later, the German jet was nowhere to be seen. The 262 pilot had not been able to hit the Mosquito, but the combat had been anything but comforting.

In June 1944, Spate had received a new assignment and was replaced as commander of JG 400's Messerschmitt 163s by Oberst Gordon Gollob. Following the invasion of France on June 6, 1944, oil became the priority target for the U.S. Strategic Air Forces in Europe. With both the Eighth and Fifteenth Air Forces striking the refineries, Gollob moved his Me 163s to Brandis near Leipzig, in southeastern Germany. From this point the limited-flight rocket craft could rise to defend the important refineries in the area of Leuna-Merseberg, Boheln, Zeitz and Luetzkendorf.

In the Merseberg area, the U.S. Army Air Force had its first encounter with the German jets. Colonel Avelin P. Tacon, Jr., Commanding Officer of the P-51-equipped 359th Fighter Group of the Eighth Air Force, was leading his unit when he encountered Me 163s: "I encountered two Me 163s. My eight P-51s were furnishing close escort for a combat wing of B-17s, and we were flying south at 25,000 feet when one of my pilots called in two contrails at six o'clock high, some five miles back, at 32,000 feet.

"I identified them immediately as jet-propelled aircraft. Their contrails could not be mistaken and looked very dense and white, somewhat like an elongated cumulus cloud that was some three-quarters of a mile in length. My section turned 180 degrees back toward the enemy fighters, which included two aircraft with jets turned on and three in a glide without jets operating at the moment.

"The two I had spotted made a diving turn to the left in close formation and feinted towards the bombers at six o'clock, cutting off their jets as they turned. Our flight turned for a head-on pass to get between them and the rear of the bomber formation. While still 3,000 yards from the bombers, they turned into us and left the bombers alone. In this turn, they banked about 80 degrees, but their course changed only about 20 degrees. Their turn radius was very large, but their rate of roll appeared excellent. Their speed, I estimated, was 500 to 600 miles per hour. Both planes passed under us, 1,000 feet below, while still in a close formation glide.

"One continued down in a 45-degree dive, the other climbed up into the sun very steeply, and I lost him. Then I looked back at the one in a dive and saw he was five miles away at 10,000 feet. Other members of my flight reported that the one that had gone up into the sun used his jet in short bursts as though it was blowing smoke rings. These pilots appeared very experienced but not aggressive. Maybe they were just on a trial flight."

The 8th Fighter Command had been waiting for the appearance of the jets for some weeks and it was no surprise when they arrived on the scene. Shortly after receiving Colonel Tacon's report, Major General William Kepner, Commanding Officer of the 8th Fighter Command, sent out a TWX message to all his command in which he reviewed Colonel Tacon's report and stated: "It is believed we can expect to see more of these aircraft immediately and that we can expect attacks on the bombers from the rear in formations or waves.

"To be able to counter and have time to turn into them, our units are going to have to be in positions relatively close to the bombers. Attention is called to the fact that probably the first thing seen will be heavy, dense contrails high and probably 30,000 feet and above, approaching rear of bombers. Jet aircraft can especially be expected in Leipzig and Munich area or any place east of nine-degree line."

From this date forward, 8th Fighter Command stressed to its leaders that their fighters stay in the proximity of the bomber formations to prevent a mass attack by Luftwaffe jet fighters.

The bombers returned to the Merseburg area on July 29, and the Army Air Force saw action with an Me 163. Riding herd on the bombers was Captain Arthur Jeffrey of the 479th Fighter Group in his Lockheed P-38 Lightning. He had just picked up a straggling B-17 from the 100th Bomb Group at about 11,000 feet over Wessermunde when a single Me 163 appeared. The rocket-powered craft made a low-side pass at the Fortress from its five o'clock position and followed through with a shallow dive. Jeffrey went after the Me 163.

The enemy craft was weaving around the Fortress when Jeffrey caught it and opened fire. He scored hits, and the 163 pilot sparked his engine and climbed to 15,000 feet. The pilot circled to the left, and the P-38 pilot turned inside of it and opened fire once more. The 163 then rolled over and went down in a split-ess maneuver that became a near-vertical dive. Jeffrey went right down behind it and continued firing, scoring some hits before the rocket craft pulled away from him. By this time, the

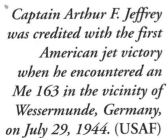

Captain Arthur F. Jeffrey was credited with the first American jet victory when he encountered an Me 163 in the vicinity of Wessermunde, Germany, on July 29, 1944. (USAF)

ENTER THE JET MENACE

Lightning pilot was trying to pull out of his dive and finally managed to come out of it about 1,500 feet, before he blacked out.

When Jeffrey recovered, he saw no sign of the Me 163. Because the 163 had taken strikes and went down in a vertical dive, Jeffrey claimed the craft either destroyed or probably destroyed. The 8th Fighter Command Victories Credits Board saw fit to award him with a destroyed credit. Years later, however, records of JG 400 did not indicate that the craft had been destroyed—it was probably only damaged. Regardless, Jeffrey had scored hits on the 163 with his .50-caliber bullets, showing that the Army Air Force was more than willing to mix it up with the new weapons of the Luftwaffe.

While Jeffrey was chasing his 163, the other two pilots in his flight continued to provide protection to the straggling B-17. They were running top cover at 16,000 feet, when another Me 163 made a pass on the bomber from out of the sun. It fired and kept right on going, diving for the clouds below at 8,000 feet. As it went down, it continued to emit smoke rings as the pilot throttled his engine. The two P-38s had no chance to pursue.

AUGUST 1944

In August, there were several sightings of Me 163s—the earliest was reported on the fifth of that month. B-17s were striking at oil targets, and Me 163s were reported in the area of the Dutch-German border, but no losses were reported. A number of other sightings of Me 163s and Me 262s were made in early August, but there seem to be no confirmations of actual damage inflicted by the new "jet menace."

The next real action came on August 16, 1944, when the American bombers went after industrial targets in central Germany. Large gaggles of Me 109s and FW 190s, along with a small number of Me 163s, rose to challenge them. Five of the Me 163s were from JG 400, and they initially flew attacks against the 305th Bomb Group. The 163 flown by Feldwebel Herbert Straznicky came in from six o'clock for a pass. He had obviously cut his power to attack, and this was his fatal mistake. Sergeant H.J. Kaysen, the tail gunner on Lieutenant D.L. Waltz's crew, opened fire on the enemy craft from 1,000 yards and continued to spray the 163 until the German pilot broke off at close range. Kaysen lost sight of the plane as it descended, but he had inflicted such damage to the rocket craft that Straznicky was forced to bail out.

Another Me 163, flown by Leutenant Hartmut Ryll, aggressively attacked the Fortress flown by Lieutenant C.J. Laverdiere and scored telling hits. The B-17's tail gunner bailed out on the first pass and one waist gunner was killed. Both inboard engines were hit, and the flaps were badly damaged. Ryll came back for another pass from below, and his fire killed the ball turret gunner and inflicted further damage to the Fortress. Certain that he had mortally damaged the B-17, Ryll left the struggling Fortress, which miraculously managed to make it back to England.

Ryll turned his attention to a straggling Fortress from the 91st Bomb Group that bore the title of *Outhouse Mouse*. As the Luftwaffe pilot maneuvered into position for his attack, he was jumped by Lieutenant Colonel John B. Murphy and his wingman, Lieutenant Cyril W. Jones, Jr., of the 359th Fighter Group, in their Mustangs. Murphy reported that the Me 163 seemed to level off, which enabled him to make a run on the rocket-powered craft. Jones related: "White Leader (Murphy) was about 1,000 feet ahead of me and about 500 feet above me on the final approach. I saw White Leader fire and strikes appeared on the tail of the E/A. White Leader broke away and I continued in, the jet A/C split-essed, and I followed him.

"I fired a short burst with a three-radi lead and observed no hits. I increased the lead and fired again. The entire canopy seemed to dissolve on the E/A, which I had identified as an Me 163. I closed very fast and broke behind him. As I passed behind the E/A, I hit his wash and did a half turn. While recovering, I blacked out and lost sight of the 163."

When Murphy completed his chandelle after he had made his pass at the 163, he sighted another Me 163 off and to his right. The

Mustang pilot closed on this craft and opened fire at 750 yards with a continuous burst. Parts peeled off the enemy aircraft and it disintegrated with a big explosion. It is quite possible that this second Me 163 that Murphy was credited with destroying was the descending plane that Straznicky had just bailed out of.

The first Me 163, which both Murphy and Jones had attacked, was that of Ryll, who was killed during the battle. JG 400 lost two Me 163s in the combat and actually downed none of the Fortresses that it had attacked.

Major Joseph Myers (right) of the 78th Fighter Group (shown here with his crew chief) and his wingman, Lieutenant Manford Croy, Jr., were credited with the destruction of the first Me 262 by U.S. Army Air Force pilots. (USAAF)

Two P-47 Thunderbolt pilots from the Eighth Air Force's 78th Fighter Group shared the first Army Air Force victory over a Messerschmitt 262 on August 28, 1944. Major Joseph Myers and his wingman, Lieutenant Manford O. Croy, Jr., were providing top cover to the rest of the group who were engaged in dive-bombing and strafing when they sighted Oberfeldwebel H. "Ronny" Lauer, of 1/KG (J) 51, headed for his base at Chievres, Belgium.

Myers reported: "While stooging around west of Brussels at 11,000 feet, I caught sight of what appeared to be a B-26, flying at about 500 feet and heading in a southerly direction, going very fast. I immediately started down to investigate and although diving at 45 degrees at 450 indicated air speed, I was no more than holding my own in regard to the unidentified aircraft.

"When approximately 5,000 feet, nearly directly over the aircraft, I could see that is was not a B-26. ... It was painted slate blue, with a long rounded nose, but I did not see any guns at this time, because he started evasive action, which consisted of small changes in direction not exceeding 90 degrees of turn. The radius of turn was very great, and although I was diving at around 450 IAS, I had very little difficulty cutting him off and causing him to change directions. He made no effort to climb or turn more than 90 degrees at any time. I closed to within 2,000 feet above him and directly astern and had full power on during a 45-degree dive in an effort to close.

"At that distance, I could readily see the similarity between the aircraft and the recognition plates of the Me 262. With full power on and the advantage of altitude, I gradually started closing on the E/A and drew up to within 500 yards astern. I was about to open fire, when the E/A cut his throttle and crash landed in a plowed field. He hit the ground just as I fired, so I continued to fire until within 100 yards of him, observing many strikes around the cockpit and jet units. It skidded over several fields and came to rest and caught fire. ... The E/A was burning brightly, giving off great clouds of black smoke. I claim one Me 262 destroyed, shared with Lieutenant M.D. Croy, Jr., my No. 4 man."

Lauer, although strafed when he fled from the aircraft, was not hit and survived to fight another day.

SEPTEMBER 1944

During September 1944, the Allies contact with the German jets was limited, but a few isolated incidents occurred. The first combat incident foretold of the hazards that photo reconnaissance aircraft

---

faced with the advent of the high-flying, speedy Me 262 jets. Lieutenant Robert Hillborn of the 7th Photo Reconnaissance Group was in his Spitfire XI when he was attacked and shot down by Leutenant Alfred Schreiber of Erprobungskommando (Ekdo) 262. Hillborn was forced to take to his parachute when the engine quit, and he descended to become a prisoner of war.

On September 11, heavy bombers from the Eighth Air Force went after oil targets in central Germany, and they were opposed by large formations of propeller-driven fighters that included Me 109s and FW 190s, as well as a small number of Me 262s. One Eighth Air Force Fighter Group that was heavily engaged was the 339th.

They met 100-plus enemy fighters in the vicinity of Annaburg, Germany, and engaged in a huge dogfight. The Mustang pilots of the 339th claimed fourteen FW 190s and Me 109s shot down. Lieutenant William A. Jones' P-51 was damaged during a strafing run and he headed for home. En route, he was engaged by an Me 262 flown by Oberfeldwebel Helmut Baudlach, who shot Jones' aircraft down. Jones joined the ranks of the prisoners of war.

The commander of the first Me 262 combat unit was Major Walter Nowotny, who was credited with more than 250 victories on the Eastern Front. Nowotny then scored at least eight victories while flying the new jet, before he was killed on November 8, 1944.

A brief encounter came two days later when eight Mustangs from the 364th Fighter Group escorted a photo reconnaissance mission. The Mustangs encountered two Me 262s, and Lieutenant John A. Walker claimed one of them damaged.

OCTOBER 1944

The Ninth Air Force got in on the jet scene on October 2, 1944, when Captain Valmore J. Beaudrault of the 365th Fighter Group had a most memorable scrap with an Me 262. Beaudrault was leading his flight on a reconnaissance mission in the Munster and Dusseldorf area, flying at about 9,000 feet, when he heard a shout from his No. 3 man, Lieutenant Robert Teeter on the R/T: "My God. What was that?"

Beaudrault looked up just in time to see a streak flash by his tail then pull up into the clouds. He immediately called his flight on the

Captain Valmore Beaudrault, of the 365th Fighter Group, evaded attacks from a KG 51 Me 262 until it was about out of fuel on October 2, 1944. He then attacked the jet, which crashed in an effort to evade at low altitude. In view of the fact that he did not fire, Beaudrault was not credited with the victory. (USAAF)

ENTER THE JET MENACE

R/T, and they went after the bogie. As they pulled up through the overcast, the flight of four found themselves alone. When the flight went back down through the clouds, Beaudrault sighted a bogie at ten o'clock, and they took off after it. Only three P-47s were left in the chase; however, one pilot had been lost in the clouds.

The Thunderbolts went down after the German jet, which pulled away from them easily, it then whipped around and came down on Beaudrault with its cannons blazing. The Thunderbolt pilot immediately pulled into a tight circle, and the jet whizzed by. The German pilot pulled up and made another pass. Once more, the P-47 pilot turned inside it. As the jet made continued passes, the combat worked its way down to the deck.

Finally, during the last pass, Beaudrault noted white puffs and the jet began to loose speed. He had either run out of fuel or had experienced flameouts of his engines. Beaudrault then pulled in on the tail of the enemy craft, which was in a long glide, and lined up to fire while the German pilot slipped from side-to-side in an attempt to throw off his aim. Just before Beaudrault hit the gun tit, the Luftwaffe pilot slipped a bit too much and one wing struck the ground, provoking a tremendous explosion. Beaudrault joined up with Teeter, and they headed for home.

Beaudrault's victim was Lauer of 1/KG (J) 51, who had attempted an unsuccessful bounce on the Ninth Air Force Thunderbolts in late August. In view of the fact that Beaudrault did not open fire on the Me 262, he was not officially credited with the victory even though he was awarded the Distinguished Flying Cross for his feat!

The 7th Photo Reconnaissance Group ran afoul of the German jets once more on October 6, 1944. One of its F-5 Lightnings was downed, and it is quite possible that it was lost to Hauptmann Georg-Peter Eder, a top Luftwaffe ace flying with Ekdo Lechfeld.

On the same day, Lieutenant C.W. Mueller of the 353rd Fighter Group reported that he had encountered two enemy jets and downed one of them during its landing approach, but nothing is officially recorded of the disposition of his claim.

In late September 1944, a number of pilots from Ekdo 262 Kommando had departed that unit to join Luftwaffe Major Walter Nowotny in his Kommando Nowotny unit, which was based at Achmer and Hesepe. This unit had become operational by early October, and on the seventh of the month, a flight from the unit attacked and probably downed several B-24s that were attacking German oil installations in the Magdeburg area.

The first American jet victory of October 7 occurred in the Osnabruck area, when Major Richard E. Conner, of the 78th Fighter Group, sighted two unidentified fighters in the vicinity of the bombers that he was escorting. He was flying at 24,000 feet, while the bogies were down about 12,000 to 14,000 feet. He and two members of his flight dove down full-bore. Conner found that he could never close on them. From their speed he realized that the bogies had to be jet aircraft.

The P-47s' pursuit paid off when the Me 262s ran short of fuel and began to circle an airfield. As Conner closed on one of the aircraft, it came back toward him in a head-on pass. The Thunderbolt pilot easily turned inside the pass and fired a ninety-degree deflection burst. The 262 then headed for the airdrome, and Conner closed rapidly when the jet lowered its landing gear. The P-47 pilot let fly with a long burst that scored many strikes on the enemy aircraft. As Conner overran the 262, his wingmen watched as it crashed on the airfield. The downed Me 262 was from 1/KG (J) 51, and although the Americans did not report it, the German pilot is said to have bailed out.

The second jet, or really the first rocket, encounter of the day came at 1230 hours when P-51 Mustangs of the 364th Fighter Group observed an Me 163 making passes at a straggling B-17. Lieutenant Elmer T. Taylor was a couple of thousand feet above the enemy when he pushed over in a dive to attack the craft. Taylor began firing from a long distance, but apparently the 163 must have run out of fuel, for suddenly he was closing very fast. At 100 yards, Taylor saw many strikes on the tail, fuselage and both wings of the Me 163. The rocket-powered craft rolled over and went straight down.

Lieutenant Willard G. Erfkamp was element leader in Taylor's flight, and he too, had gone down on the Me 163. When Taylor saw that he was going to overrun the enemy plane, he called for Erfkamp to follow it. The Mustang pilot did, placing further telling hits into the craft before it landed in a grass field.

Erfkamp and his wingman pulled up, made a wing-over and came back to strafe the Me 163 on the ground. The pilot, Husser, survived.

The Me 163s of JG 400 put in one of their most strenuous and successful missions of the war that day. Its pilots successfully downed at least two B-17s and damaged several others, but in the course of the action they lost three Me 163s, with one pilot killed and two wounded.

The next combat of the day involved Lieutenant Urban "Ben" Drew of the 361st Fighter Group, who was leading his squadron

Lieutenant Urban L. Drew of the 361st Fighter Group downed two Me 262s when he caught them taking off from Achmer airdrome on October 7, 1944. His P-51 Mustang Detroit Miss *(shown opposite page) documents his victories on its canopy rail. Drew received a belated Air Force Cross for his victories in 1983.* (Drew)

that day, and two pilots from Kommando Nowotny, based at Achmer. Drew attempted to get involved in a fight that had broken out behind the bombers he was escorting, but upon his arrival the fight had dissipated and he could find no action. He joined up with a formation of B-17s and stayed with them until he sighted two aircraft on the airfield at Achmer.

Drew reported: "I watched them for a while and saw one of them start to taxi. The lead ship was in take-off position on the east-west runway, and the taxiing ship got into position for a formation take-off. I waited until they were both airborne, then I rolled over from 15,000 feet and headed for the attack with my flight behind me.

"I caught up with the second Me 262 when he was about 1,000 feet off the ground. I was indicating 450 MPH, and the jet aircraft could not have been going faster than 200 MPH. I started firing from about 400 yards, thirty-degrees deflection, and as I closed on him, I observed hits all over the wings and fuselage. Just as I passed him, I saw a sheet of flame burst out near the right wing root. As I glanced back, I saw a gigantic explosion and a sheet of red-orange flame that shot out over an area of about 1,000 feet.

ENTER THE JET MENACE

"The other jet aircraft was about 500 yards ahead of me and had started a fast climbing turn to the left. I was still indicating about 400 MPH, and I had to haul back on the stick to stay with him. I started shooting from about sixty-degrees deflection, at 300 yards, and my bullets were just hitting the tail section of the enemy aircraft. I kept horsing back on the stick, and my bullets crept up the fuselage to the cockpit.

"Just then, the canopy flew off in two sections, and the plane rolled over and went into a flat spin. The aircraft hit the ground on its back at about a sixty-degree angle. I did not see the pilot bail out, and the enemy aircraft exploded violently. As I looked back at the two wrecks, I saw two mounting columns of black smoke."

As far as is known, the pilots involved in this combat were Oberleutnant Paul Bley and Leutnant Gerhard Kobert. Kobert is reported to have been killed when his aircraft exploded, and Bley is said to have survived a parachute jump, which would seem impossible.

Drew had thought that his victories would have been confirmed by his wingman, Lieutenant Robert McCandliss. However, instead of staying with Drew, McCandliss had flown off on his own to attack some flak batteries and gotten himself shot down. McCandliss was taken prisoner after bailing out.

Years later, Drew's victories were completely confirmed by Eder, the Luftwaffe flying ace from Ekdo Lechfeld, who had witnessed the combat. Originally, Drew had been awarded the Distinguished Flying Cross for his feat, but in 1983 he was awarded the Air Force Cross.

As illustrated by the combats of early October, the American pilots had learned that they could easily turn inside the German jets, which is what they did to survive. To protect the bombers, the fighters knew they would have to stay close to their charges and maintain an altitude advantage. From this advantage, the fighters could dive down on any jet or rocket-powered attackers and break up their formations. As far as air-to-air combat went, however, the American fighters could not convince the Me 262s to stay and fight them unless they were so outnumbered they could be boxed in. The jets possessed such a speed advantage that they could break off combat any time they desired.

More and more, the leaders of the Eighth Air Force fighter unit escorts began to pore over maps to locate the fields from which the jets were operating. At these locations, the Me 262s and Me 163s were completely vulnerable. The 262s were slow to take off, and it took them precious minutes to build up airspeed once they got off the ground. Also, their endurance in the air was limited.

The Me 262 could carry only about forty-five minutes of fuel, and the Me 163 was only good for about eight minutes of sustained rocket power. Once their fuel had been depleted, the Me 163 and Me 262 were forced to head for their fields immediately. As they let down over their bases, they had no choice but to land. By that time, they did not have sufficient fuel left to rise, fight for a few minutes and return. American and British fighter pilots both knew this weakness and used these tactics more frequently as the end of the war drew near.

This Me 262 shows markings similar to those used on the jets assigned to Kommando Nowotny. (AFM via Ethell)

ENTER THE JET MENACE

On October 15, P-47s of the 78th Fighter Group had a chance to polish their tactics when they met Me 262s from 1/JG (J) 51 while escorting heavy bombers to targets in the Cologne area. Lieutenant Hugh O. Foster engaged one of the jets in the Bohmte area and managed to score some strikes on it, but he only claimed the aircraft as damaged. However, the jet sustained enough damage that the pilot was forced to make a crash landing.

One pilot in the 78th Group, Lieutenant Huie H. Lamb, Jr., was just about ready to head for home when he spotted an Me 262 in the area of Osnabruck. Lamb was flying at approximately 14,000 feet, which put him in good position to dive down on his prey, which flew at around 5,000 feet. Lamb dove down in the heavy Thunderbolt, building up speed all the way. The P-47 was doing about 475 MPH when he closed the distance to about 1,000 yards, then Lamb hit his water injection in order to close the gap further.

Once he was in range, Lamb opened fire and the jet turned to the left. This was a fatal mistake. The Thunderbolt easily turned inside it, which gave Lamb a good, close target, on which he immediately bestowed numerous strikes. As a last resort, the Luftwaffe pilot, Feldwebel Edgar Junghans, led the P-47 over his airfield where the flak batteries forced Lamb away with their concentration of fire. However, it was too late, Junghans' aircraft was blazing by the time he managed to bring it in for a crash landing. The pilot succumbed to his injuries a few days later.

NOVEMBER 1944

The next shooting encounter between American fighter pilots and German jets did not occur until November 1. Mustangs of the 20th and 352nd Fighter Groups, plus P-47s of the 56th Fighter Group were escorting bombers to targets at Gelsenkirchen when, over Holland, four Me 262s from Kommando Nowotny attacked them. Oberfeldwebel Willi Banzhaff bounced the Yellow Flight of the 20th Fighter Group and downed Lieutenant Denis J. Alison's aircraft before anyone really realized what was going on. Banzhaff continued his dive, attracting more attention than he had ever dreamed of.

Mustangs from the 20th, particularly Lieutenant Richard Flowers, flew in hot pursuit of the German. As Banzhaff's 262 flashed by the 352nd Fighter Group, he also drew a number of those American fighters into the fray. As the covey of cats continued to pursue the mouse, a few Thunderbolts from the 56th Fighter Group entered the chase, too.

Flowers pursued until he was pulling seventy-two inches of mercury at 3,000 RPM, and although he opened fire and claimed hits on the jet, he was to receive no credit when Banzhaff was forced to bail out. The two pilots who split the victory were Lieutenants William T. Gerbe, Jr., of the 352nd Fighter Group, and Lieutenant Walter R. Groce of the 56th Fighter Group.

Gerbe stated that he had more speed than his element leader and that he was going for the jet. As he described the subsequent events: "The Me 262 made a turn into me. I turned with him and it put me

Captain Fred W. Glover, of the 4th Fighter Group, is shown with his Mustang, in which he downed an Me 163 in the vicinity of Leipzig on November 2, 1944. (USAAF)

ENTER THE JET MENACE

right on his tail. I was using the K-14 Gyro Gunsight and first opened fire at 200 yards. I saw hits in the tail section, closing up to about 150 yards, and shot out his right jet as he was climbing to leave me behind. After I shot out his right jet, the Me 262 went into a flat spin to the right, and the pilot bailed out a few seconds later."

Groce was able to open fire on the Me 262 from slightly below and apparently his gun camera film must have shown good strikes as well—he was awarded half the victory.

After a brief absence, JG 400 was back in the thick of things on November 2, 1944. At least eleven Me 163s rose from their base at Brandis to oppose bombers striking oil targets in central Germany. Captain Fred W. Glover was leading the 4th Fighter Group when he sighted a contrail climbing rapidly toward the bomber stream. The German craft pulled up level with the bombers at 25,000 feet and turned back toward the bomber stream in a slight dive. Glover dropped his auxiliary tanks and headed for the 163 on a convergence course.

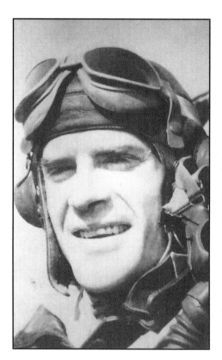

As the rocket-powered craft crossed in front of his P-51, Glover made a quick ninety-degree turn and fell in behind the Me 163. He quickly opened fire and registered strikes all over the tail, wings and cockpit of the craft from 400 yards, and the belly of the aircraft exploded. Glover overshot, and as he looked back, he could see that

Captain Louis H. Norley of the 4th Fighter Group, also credited with an Me 163 on November 2, 1944, flew a colorful Mustang named Red Dog XII *(shown opposite page).* (USAAF)

the tail was all but shot off the craft and its canopy was badly damaged. Glover pulled up to look for another target as the Me 163 went plunging down. One of his flight called to report that the pilot, Oberfeldwebel Gunther Andreas, had bailed out.

Meanwhile, Captain Louis H. Norley was leading the 335th Fighter Squadron of the 4th Fighter Group when he spied an Me 163 dropping down at his six o'clock position. As soon as he dumped his drop tanks, Norley set his new K-14 sight and went full-throttle after his target, which was just a little out of range.

Norley got on the tail of the 163 and followed it down. As the rocket-powered craft began to pull away, the Mustang pilot fired a few short bursts, hoping that craft would turn, and sure enough, it did. As the 163 went into a port turn, its speed fell off considerably. Norley related: "I closed on him rapidly. I was using a K-14 sight for the first time … however, I did get a couple of strikes on the tail, firing from 250 to fifty yards. My speed was around 450 MPH when I got into range. I throttled back, but was unable to stay in the turn with him due to excessive speed. I overshot him, pulled up and got on his tail again.

ENTER THE JET MENACE

43

"Up to this time, he had not been using his blower, at least he was not emitting any black smoke. As I closed on him the second time, he punched on his blower for a couple of seconds and then cut it off again. I closed to 400 yards … fired again and saw strikes on the tail. The 163 rolled over and plummeted straight down from 8,000 feet with fire flashing intermittently from his port side and exhaust. He slammed in a small village and the aircraft exploded."

His victim was Oberfeldwebel Jacob Bollenrath, who perished in the crash.

Other Me 163s continued to attack B-17s from the 388th and the 91st Bomb Groups. Oberfeldwebel Horst Rolly was killed in combat with these bombers, and it is quite likely that he fell to one of the gunners from the 388th Bomb Group, who claimed one Me 163 destroyed and one probably destroyed.

Another Me 163 pilot was reported missing at the end of the day, who may also have fallen victim to gunners from either the 388th or the 91st Bomb Group. A few days later, the body of Feldwebel Straznicky was found in the cockpit of his Me 163.

On November 4, during an escort mission to the Hanover area, Thunderbolts of the 356th Fighter Group were attacked by Me 262s from Kommando Nowotny. Captain Dick Rann, of the 359th Fighter Squadron, claimed one of the jets damaged but Flight Officer Willard W. Royer of the 360th Fighter Squadron was hit and crashed to his death in the Dummer Lake area following a pass from an Me 262 flown by Oberfeldwebel Gobel.

The 357th and 361st Fighter Groups escorted the "Big Friends" to the Minden, Germany, area on November 6. Leading White Flight in the 363rd Fighter Squadron of the 357th Group was Captain Charles E. "Chuck" Yeager, who would gain postwar fame as the first man to exceed the speed of sound.

Yeager sighted a flight of three Me 262s, which were from Kommando Nowotny. He took his flight down to try to head off the last man in the formation. He managed to punch in a ninety-degree deflection shot but scored no real results. The jets used their superior speed to hustle out of the area.

The Mustangs now flew at 5,000 feet, and Yeager spotted the jets once more, going down in a split-ess. Pulling seventy-five inches of manifold pressure and indicating 430 MPH, the P-51 dove into firing range. Yeager managed to score hits on the fuselage and wings of a 262 from 300 yards before the jet pulled away and was lost in haze.

After climbing back up to 8,000 feet, Yeager spied an airfield below with big, wide runways and began to circle it. A little flak began to come up, but it was wide of the mark. Yeager spotted a lone Me 262 heading for the south end of the airfield at 500 feet. The jet was throttled back and the Mustang pilot had no trouble closing; he went down after it indicating 500 MPH.

As he closed, the flak began to fly thick and fast, but Yeager managed to get off a short burst at 400 yards that registered hits on the wings of the enemy. Yeager broke off the combat at 300 yards, for the flak was really getting heavy. As he broke straight up, he glanced back and watched the 262 crash land in a wooded field, snapping one of its wings off.

About half an hour later in the area of Bassum, Lieutenant

Future test pilot, Captain Charles E. "Chuck" Yeager shot up then rode down an Me 262 on November 6, 1944. His victory was the first of many accomplished by 357th Group pilots. (USAAF)

William J. Quinn, of the 361st Fighter Group, sighted a duo of Me 262s to the left and above the bombers that he was escorting. As soon as the Mustangs went after them, the jets made a pass at the bombers from seven o'clock, then they sped away before the P-51s could close on them.

As the Mustangs climbed to 10,000 feet, another pair of 262s was spotted down at 6,000 feet. Quinn and his flight went after them, but as soon as the jets saw the Mustangs, they turned east and headed for home. They were leaving the Mustangs behind, when they went into a turn to the left. The Mustang on Quinn's left opened fire on one, causing the 262 pilot to reverse his direction and turn back to the right, which brought him right across Quinn's nose.

The P-51 immediately opened fire with a thirty-degree deflection shot, but he scored no hits. The desperate Luftwaffe pilot throttled forward to escape, but Quinn, who was turning inside, hit him with two good bursts along the fuselage and canopy. The Me 262 began to smoke, went into a spiral and continued earthwards from 2,000 feet, enveloped in smoke and flames.

November 8, 1944, proved to be a momentous day for the Luftwaffe. Although several victories were scored by the Me 262s, three jet aircraft assigned to the Nowotny Kommando were lost. While two of the pilots managed to bail out, the unit's leader, Major Walter Nowotny, holder of the Knights Cross with Oakleaves and Swords and Diamonds and with more than 250 aerial victories, was lost.

Leutenant Franz Schall and Feldwebel Buttner were airborne for the first encounter of the day, as Eighth Air Force B-17s headed for the oil refinery installations at Merseburg. Each of the pilots had claimed victories over American fighters on their subsequent return to base. Shortly thereafter, Nowotny, Schall and Oberfeldwebel Baudach were airborne as Generalleutnant Adolph Galland, who was visiting for the day, looked on.

Schall bounced Thunderbolts from Green Flight, of the 359th Fighter Squadron, 356th Fighter Group, damaging the aircraft flown by Lieutenant Charles C. McKelvy. Lieutenant Edward G. Rudd immediately turned and fired at the jet but made no strikes. Schall turned, came back at the P-47s and fired at McKelvy once more. He also hit Lieutenant William L. Hoffert, who was forced to bail out immediately. McKelvy attempted to make it to Belgium, but he fell victim to Me 109s en route and was forced to crash land in Germany, where he became a prisoner of war.

Earlier, Lieutenant Warren Corwin, of the 357th Fighter Group, had experienced engine trouble with his Mustang. Lieutenant James W. Kenney had left his formation to escort Corwin home. As the two cruised along, they sighted a box of B-17s with no escort and decided to fly cover for them.

The two Mustangs climbed up to 22,000 feet, where they spied a bogie headed for the bombers. When the P-51s broke into it, they discovered it was an Me 262, apparently Schall. The jet made a pass

A still image from one of the gun cameras installed in Allied aircraft shows an Me 163 being attacked by a P-51 Mustang. (USAAF)

ENTER THE JET MENACE

on the bombers from ten o'clock, then came back from five o'clock. Kenney got on the tail of the jet and fired from 400 yards, coaxing a puff of smoke from the 262, which went into a dive. Corwin split-essed to follow it down.

Kenney then went down after the enemy craft as well, which was diving slowly, causing the Mustang pilot to overshoot him twice. The Me 262 then went into a turn to the left, which was a mistake. Kenney turned inside and wound up at six o'clock to the 262. Firing from 250 yards to dead astern, smoke began to pour out of the right engine nacelle and the pilot, Schall, bailed out.

During this combat, Corwin had disappeared. It is possible that after he split-essed, his dive velocity was faster than that of the slow-diving 262 and that he wound up in front of the four 30 MM guns of the jet. It is known that he was shot up and badly wounded by a German jet pilot, for he called out his condition over the R/T and was heard by two pilots from his group.

Flying a P-51 with the 384th Fighter Squadron of the 364th Fighter Group, Lieutenant Richard W. Stevens, was escorting bombers home from the Merseberg bombing mission. He received a call over the R/T that the bombers were under attack. Cruising at 20,000 feet, Stevens saw an Me 262 diving under him with about a dozen Mustangs in pursuit. Stevens and his wingman, Lieutenant Richard J. O'Connor, split-essed and joined the chase. The jet seemingly outdistanced all of its pursuers and took refuge in the clouds at 7,000 feet, going east.

Suddenly, the Me 262 reappeared. It had made a 180-degree turn to the left that brought it toward Stevens. The Mustang pilot maneuvered in behind the Me 262 and gave it a two-second burst from 500 yards. The P-51 was flying full-bore, and Stevens noted several instrument readings over the red line markings.

He also had a tendency to skid in his pursuit, which he later found out was due to one inboard gun that was not firing. The jet began to slow, and Stevens hit it with another two-second burst, then a longer burst that scored numerous strikes. The Me 262's left jet engine seemed to loose power.

In a last desperate attempt to escape, the Me 262 pilot led Stevens over an airfield where flak sprang up through the overcast. Stevens continued to fire until all his ammunition was gone and observed numerous further strikes on the jet, which went into a steep left-hand turn, then went down into the heavy overcast. All of this was observed by O'Connor, who had followed Stevens over the airfield and run into heavy flak. Because neither Stevens nor his wingman had actually seen the jet crash, the claim was initially entered as a damaged.

Earlier, Nowotny had called to report that he had downed a bomber and a fighter. Minutes later, his final transmissions came into the ground station at Nowotny's field at Achmer stating that he was trying to make it home and that he had been hit. A few moments later, his Me 262 came out of the overcast vertically and crashed into a meadow, where it exploded.

When 8th Fighter Command evaluated the claims for the day, they came across claims from Captain Ernest C. Fiebelkorn, of the 20th Fighter Group, and Lieutenant Edward B. Haydon, of the 357th Fighter Group, both of whom had been involved in a chase of an Me 262 that had seemed to be out of control. The Mustang pilots had chased the craft over Achmer airfield, and it had pulled up into the overcast, rolled over on its back and crashed into the ground.

Even though neither pilot fired a shot, they were awarded credit for the destruction of the Me 262. This destroyed Me 262 may well have been the abandoned aircraft of Schall plunging out of control to earth.

Later, Stevens' claim for an Me 262 damaged was confirmed as destroyed. Even his Intelligence Officer noted on his encounter report: "After checking all Eighth Fighters' MERs ... I believe the Me 262 seen destroyed by the 357 FG and the 20 FG A and B Groups was the plane that Lieutenant Stevens destroyed."

However, this still does not account for the crash of two aircraft in the immediate vicinity. After, the reassessment of Stevens' claim, there can be practically no doubt that he is the pilot who downed Nowotny.

Stevens, fifty years later, describes himself as never being an aspiring ace, but just a young fighter pilot trying to do his job and finish up his tour so he could go home. He had no inkling of the stature of the pilot he had downed. When asked if he realized that he had shot down Major Walter Nowotny, Stevens asked, "Who in hell was he?"

Some distance away from the airfield at Achmer, a third Me 262 was downed whose pilot may have been Baudach, the Oberfeldwebel who had taken off with Schall and Nowotny. Lieutenant Anthony Maurice of the 375th Fighter Squadron, 361st Fighter Group, was

From all information available, it would seem that the victor over the legendary Major Walter Nowotny was Lieutenant Richard W. Stevens, of the 364th Fighter Group, who downed an Me 262 over Achmer on November 8, 1944, that was later identified as Nowotny's. (Stevens)

four miles west of Meppel, Germany, at 1230 hours when he saw a contrail diving down in front of him. He called it out to his flight leader and started to follow it with the rest of his flight. As they went down from 18,000 feet, the bogie was identified as an Me 262, and it began to pull away from them.

They spotted a second aircraft, and as they broke—one right and one left—Maurice went after the one to the left. The Mustang pilot had the altitude advantage, and he opened fire, giving it good lead from 400 yards. Hits were observed on the fuselage, and Maurice sucked back on the stick to stay in firing position. By this time, the jet had slowed down, and as he was about to open fire again, Maurice saw the pilot bail out from 5,000 feet. The aircraft continued down, smashed into the earth and exploded.

The second aircraft, which had broken to the right, proved to be a P-51 that had been under attack by the Me 262.

Following the death of Nowotny, Hauptman Eder was appointed the commander of the Kommando. The unit was redesignated 3/EJG 2 and moved to Lechfeld airfield. Shortly thereafter, its pilots became the nucleus of 3/JG 7, which became the dominant interceptor unit flying the Me 262 and the primary opposition to the American bomber streams in Europe for the rest of World War II.

On November 18, more than 400 Eighth Air Force fighters participated in strafing sweeps over German. The 4th and the 353rd Fighter Groups went after the Me 262 base at Leipheim. The 4th Group claimed a dozen jets destroyed on the ground, while the 353rd claimed one. Two jets were caught in the air, and one was destroyed by Captain John C. Fitch and Lieutenant John M. Creamer of the 4th.

Creamer was flying No. 3 position in his flight, with Fitch as No. 4. The Mustangs arrived at the enemy airfield flying at 5,000 feet, and Creamer spotted an Me 262 at 4,500 feet heading south. The jet was throttled back to about 230 MPH and the two P-51s had no trouble closing on it. Creamer opened fire using his K-14 Gyro

Gunsight from 800 yards. The pilot of the jet jumped on the throttle, but he was hit hard before he could escape. The nose of the 262 dropped, and it went into a shallow dive as Creamer closed to 350 yards.

As the jet went into a turn, Fitch turned inside it and opened fire at 300 yards, getting strikes on its engines, wing roots and fuselage. Fitch broke off at point-blank range when the aircraft reached 500 feet. The jet went into a right-hand turn, and Creamer hit him again with a short burst. The 262 crashed and exploded.

Major Georg-Peter Eder took over command of Kommando Nowotny following Nowotny's death and later became commander of 9 Staffel of Jagdgeschwader 7. Eder claimed at least fifteen victories while flying the Me 262.

For the remainder of November, there were no encounters of note between American fighters and German jets. German jet pilots made several claims over American fighters, but these cannot be pinpointed. During this time, however, a few American photo reconnaissance aircraft were intercepted, and one of the high-flying, unarmed pilots met with disaster.

On November 26, Oberfeldwebel Hermann Buchner intercepted an F-5 from the 7th Photo Reconnaissance Group that was headed for Stuttgart. Buchner downed Lieutenant Irvin J. Rickey before the American pilot knew he was under attack. Rickey was able to bail out of his flaming aircraft and became a prisoner of war after floating down into enemy territory in his parachute.

On that same day, Major Rudi Sinner intercepted an F-5 and its three P-38 escorts. The F-5 was near Munich, when its pilot noticed the German jet coming after him. The F-5 dropped its wing tanks and broke into the 262, and as Sinner came around for another attack, he was met by the escorting P-38s. Sinner went into a dive to escape, and he finally squeaked by when the P-38s broke off combat to join back up with their photo recee aircraft. Determined to get a kill, Sinner ascended again and attacked the four aircraft from below. He hit and downed one of the escorting P-38s, which was flown by Lieutenant Julius Thomas, who bailed out and was taken prisoner.

DECEMBER 1944

The 3/JG 7 unit continued its activities from Lechfeld and initiated jet action on December 2, when Leutenant Weber of that unit attacked an F-5 from the Italy-based 5th Photo Group. Weber was

An Me 262 sits on an apparently snow-covered field. The jets flew some overflights of the American lines but saw little air-to-air combat during the Battle of the Bulge. (via Ethell)

ENTER THE JET MENACE

hit by one of the P-51s from the 325th Fighter Group that was escorting the recee aircraft, but he still managed to score some hits on his prey. The jet then made a head-on pass at Lieutenant Walter A. Hinson, who was flying the other Mustang escort. Hinson got some hits on the 262, which broke off and quickly outdistanced its foes.

On December 9, Lieutenant Harry L. Edwards, of the 486th Fighter Squadron, of the 352nd Fighter Group, caught Stabsfeldwebel Hans Zander of 4/KG (J) 51 at 29,000 feet in the vicinity of Kircheim, Germany. Edwards broke behind the jet and gave it a long burst from maximum range. Luckily, he scored a number of hits, and as the Luftwaffe pilot attempted to go to full-throttle and get away, he found one of his engines inoperative. The 262 pilot headed for the deck, and Edwards stayed with him, following about 300 yards to the rear.

When they reached 500 feet, the jet leveled off and Edwards opened fire from 300 yards. The first burst hit the left jet engine, knocking out what little power the Me 262 pilot was getting from it. The Mustang pilot then closed to point-blank range and proceeded to shoot large chunks off the aircraft, which was now smoking and headed earthwards. As Edwards pulled up, the jet crashed to the ground and exploded in two large sheets of flame.

Mid-December brought on the worst winter that northern Europe had experienced in years, setting the stage for the massive German panzer offensive through Belgium and Luxembourg that would become known as the infamous Battle of the Bulge. While Allied aircraft were grounded by the horrible weather, the Germans launched an ambitious attempt to drive their tanks into the port of Antwerp and split the Allied front in northern Europe.

The Antwerp offensive failed—much to the good fortune of the Allies. This failure was due to the dogged tenacity of American ground forces and to a break in the weather that enabled Allied fighters, transports and bombers to take to the skies, destroying the enemy and supplying ground troops that had been stranded for days with little ammunition or food.

The German jets engaged in little activity during this time. About the only bit of action occurred in the south of Germany as Me 262s made several attempts to intercept American F-5 photo recee aircraft. One battle took place northwest of Passau, near the Austrian-German border, when P-51 Mustangs from the 31st Fighter Group, of the Fifteenth Air Force, were escorting a high-altitude recee mission. Two of the Mustang pilots were Lieutenant Eugene P. McGlauflin and Flight Officer Roy L. Scales. "I probably saw the jet before any of the others," said McGlauflin. "All of a sudden, I looked up and almost right in front of me was this stranger. I called on the R/T, 'Roy, is that you?'

" 'Hell no.' was the reply, and then someone called out, 'It's a jet-propelled!' I sent the rest of my flight with the recee plane we were escorting, then with my wingman, Scales, I took on the jet job. Neither of us had any idea that we would shoot him down. In fact, I called Scales and remarked, 'Isn't this a lot of fun?'

" 'It sure is,' he replied as we turned with the jet.

"Three times the Jerry dove down, then pulled up in a wide sweeping turn to the left. I was very much surprised to find that my Mustang could gain a little in the dives. After the first time, I took a chance that he would pull left every time he climbed, and sure enough, he did.

"Every time he started to climb, I cut inside him, and because my circles were smaller, I could climb with him. So, I came quite close—within 800 yards—and each time he crossed my sight shot. I didn't see any hits, but at that distance, it's doubtful you could see hits anyhow.

"I was shooting at him, too," commented Scales. "On his third climb he started a level turn at 28,000 feet and almost headed into me. I was only 250 to 300 yards away and shot at him with about a twenty-degree deflection. I saw what seemed to be red flashes coming off one nacelle and wing.

ENTER THE JET MENACE

"He leveled off for a moment or two, then started a dive. As he got to about 5,000 feet, he leveled off again, and smoke—quite a bit of brown smoke—started coming out. The pilot bailed out. We were diving right on his tail. ... When I landed, my crew chief remarked that the paint on my Mustang was wrinkled, which means that the wings had buckled a little."

The following day, another F-5 fell victim to a German jet. Mustangs of the 353rd Fighter Group were escorting two F-5s on a recee mission, when they were suddenly hit by an Me 262 from 3/JG 7, which was flown by Oberfeldwebel Buttner. One of the F-5s was downed while Captain H.D. Stump and Lieutenant S.E. Stevenson pursued the jet down to 15,000 feet. Each took a shot at the jet and claimed to have damaged it.

On Christmas Eve, F-5s of the 7th Photo Recee Group were attacked once more. Two of the aircraft took off from Valenciennes, France, on a mapping mission over Germany. In the vicinity of Nurnberg, they were attacked by two Me 262s, which badly damaged the aircraft flown by Lieutenant I.J. Purdy. As he limped along on one engine, Purdy was saved from bailing out by his partner, Lieutenant Robert N. Florine, who made repeated head-on runs at the jets, even though he was unarmed.

After two hours of single-engine flight, Purdy finally made it back to base and completed a successful belly landing. The aircraft was a total wash-out, but Purdy escaped injury. His savior, Florine, made it back to base without further incident.

On December 21, 1944, a German unit, 9/KG 76, equipped with the new Arado 234 jet bombers, arrived at Meunster-Handorf airdrome. That unit flew the first jet bomber mission on December 24. The following day, they made shallow diving attacks on Liege, Belgium.

December 31 marked the first combat encounter with an Arado 234 jet bomber. Lieutenant Colonel John C. Meyer, of the 352nd Fighter Group, was leading the 328th Fighter Squadron in the vicinity of Vilviers flying at 6,000 feet, when an Arado 234 heading northeast was sighted. The Arado was attacked by Captain Donald Bryan, who scored some good hits on the starboard engine of the craft. Another Ar 234 was then sighted underneath Bryan, at his six o'clock. Unaware that there was no forward firing armament on the aircraft, Meyer called for Bryan to break, and he gave chase until the jet pulled up into the overcast.

Meyer reported: "I climbed up through overcast and spotted the target at eleven o'clock to me and heading sixty degrees. Since I was between the target aircraft and the Rhine, I continued chase. I seemed to be neither gaining nor losing ground, pulling sixty-seven

Lieutenant Colonel John C. Meyer of the 352nd Fighter Group, was credited with downing an Ar 234, which he attacked near Kirchheim on December 31, 1944. (USAF)

ENTER THE JET MENACE

inches and 3,000 RPM. Just west of Bonn, the enemy aircraft went back into the clouds, and I went under also, losing sight of him. I continued on this heading and again sighted the enemy in a port turn at 5,000 feet, above the the undercast, with its tops at 3,000 to 4,000 feet. I was able to close and fired two, two-second bursts at 700 and 600 yards, thirty-degrees deflection.

"I observed no strikes, but the enemy pilot jettisoned his canopy (or escape hatch). To avoid going into clouds in a vertical bank, I broke off the attack and momentarily lost sight of him. A few seconds later, swinging around a small cumulus cloud top, I saw the enemy aircraft headed straight down and it disappeared into the overcast at 3,000 feet."

As 1944 came to a close, the Allies fully realized that the jet menace would increase during the new year and they were taking measures to compensate for it. Generals Spaatz and Doolittle were concerned, particularly about the Messerschmitt 262, for it presented the biggest challenge to the bombers.

There was no doubt that the Me 262 was much faster than the American fighters of the day, and the Americans had no new jet fighter that was competitive and near ready for combat. Meanwhile, American fighter units were to keep close tabs on the German airfields that housed the jets and make every attempt to either catch the aircraft as they rose for combat or pounce on them when they were returning home low on fuel.

The Luftwaffe had already based numerous Focke Wulf 190D fighters in the area of the Me 262 bases to counteract this action, but the superior numbers of American aircraft made protecting the German aircraft difficult. In an attempt to catch as many of the jets as they could on the ground, American heavy bombers flew numerous strikes against the German airfields. They also bombed the factories where the jets were being made, but they would not learn until after the war how well-disbursed the manufacturing of the Me 262 was or know the quantities of the craft that were being produced.

The bomber crews were quite apprehensive and hoped that they would not encounter the jets, but the fighter pilots considered the Me 262 a challenge and continually plotted tactics against it. Enough Me 262s had already been encountered for the Mustang pilots to learn they could easily outturn the 262 and they could out-climb it at low altitude.

On the other hand, they knew the jets could easily pull away from them with their superior speed, and its 30 MM armament was lethal. It took only a couple of 30 MM hits to pretty well put a P-51 out of commission, and even a B-17 could be downed with five of six rounds of 30 MM. The Mustang pilots worked on using their superior numbers to box the 262 in, thus defeating its speed superiority, then they would down it through their maneuverability.

In the coming months of 1945, the jet challenge intensified drastically and combat with the Me 262 become more and more frequent.

The Ar 234 relied on its speed for defense. A few had remote firing rearward guns, but most did not, and most American fighter pilots were unaware that this model possessed no forward firing armament. (via Ethell)

ENTER THE JET MENACE

CHAPTER 3

THE MENACE GROWS

New Year's morning, 1945, the Luftwaffe flew its final massive strike against Allied airpower in northern Europe. More than 800 fighters took off at dawn to participate in Operation Bodenplatte, which struck at Royal Air Force and American bases in Holland and Belgium in an attempt to destroy Allied air superiority on the Continent. Somewhere around 150 Allied aircraft were destroyed on various air bases.

However, the losses the Luftwaffe suffered during the operation were disastrous, and these losses broke the back of the vaunted German Air Force. The Germans lost about 300 aircraft, many of which fell to their own unwarned flak batteries. One hundred fifty-one German pilots were killed or missing and another sixty-three taken prisoner. The most crippling losses of the operation, though, were the four Geschwaderkommodores, five Gruppenkommandeures and eleven Staffenkaptaines lost due to the Allies.

Twenty-one Me 262s from 1/KG (J) 51 participated in Operation Bodenplatte by strafing two airfields in Holland. The exact damage they inflicted is not known, and no record exists of the losses suffered by the unit during their phase of the operation.

Later in the day, heavy bombers from the Eighth Air Force struck at oil refineries in central Germany. Lieutenant Franklin W. Young was a part of the escort force that the 4th Fighter Group sent up. Young and his 336th Fighter Squadron encountered a few Me 109s in the target area and during the ensuing scrap, the Mustang pilot blew one Me 109 up after a brief encounter.

As the squadron formed back up and headed for home, Young spotted a bogie flying 2,000 feet above and on a course that was coming in at ninety degrees to the Mustangs. Young was given permission to investigate, so he and his wingman began to climb. The two P-51s had just reached a position above it, when the bogie went into a slow turn to the left. Young cut inside him and closed enough to identify the aircraft as an Me 262.

Young recalled: "I started down on him, and he peeled off to the left and started down. I caught him at 3,000 feet and opened fire from line astern. I observed strikes in the tail and trailing edges of his wing and belly. I also observed pieces flying off. He pulled up and went into a steep spiral. When the plane hit the ground, it exploded. The pilot did not get out."

A few days after Operation Bodenplatte, 3/JG 7 changed bases. The Staff and the 11 Staffel unit went to Brandenburg/Briest; the 9 Staffel unit, under Hauptman Georg-Peter Eder, went to Parchim; and Oberleutnant Franz Schall with the 10 Staffel unit moved to Oranienburg.

January 13, 1945

No further combat occurred between the U.S. Army Air Force and the German jets until January 13. On that day, Lieutenant Walter J. Konantz and his 338th Fighter Squadron, from the 55th Fighter Group, went after the airdrome at Giebelstadt. They had just arrived over the field when Konantz observed three or four aircraft taxiing along the long runway. The Mustang pilots circled a few minutes to give the jets from 1/KG (J) 51 time to begin to take off.

Konantz reported: "One of the jets took off on the long runway from east to west, made a climbing port turn and came back east at about 1,000 feet south of the airdrome. I was on the same side of the field, above him, and going in the opposite direction.

"I made a tight 180-degree turn and identified him as an Me 262. I caught him easily as he was in a medium turn and got a long burst into him from 200 yards. He caught fire near the port jet unit and made a diving turn straight into the ground about a half mile from the airdrome. He exploded with a big flash of flame when he hit."

The "Big Friends" of the Eighth Air Force went back after oil refineries on January 14, and the Luftwaffe rose to oppose them. The 353rd Fighter Group had taken the bombers in to the target at Derbin and was on its way out when two Me 262s were sighted headed north at 10,000 feet. Lawyer Red Flight, from the 351st Fighter Squadron, was at 20,000 feet, and they pounced down out of the sun at full-throttle. Lieutenant Billy J. Murray led the bounce. He picked out the 262 on the left, opened fire as soon as he was in range and scored hits on its right engine. The jet pulled up sharply and the pilot, Unteroffizier Detjens of 9/JG 7, bailed out.

Lieutenants James W. Rohrs and George J. Rosen got after the other Me 262. Rohrs reported: "My flight leader (Lieutenant Murray) took the one on the left, and I took the one on the right. I fired a one-second burst observing smoke and fire from the right wing root and jet nacelle. The aircraft being attacked by Murray broke sharply to the right in front of me, and I had to break in the same direction to avoid a mid-air collision. In doing so, I was forced to break off combat with the jet I was firing at, but it also put me in a good position to attack the one that had broken in front of me.

"I gave him a short burst before I noticed that the pilot had already bailed out. I then completed my 360-degree turn to the right and started out after the other jet, which had been damaged sufficiently by my first burst to keep him from outrunning me. I closed to 700 yards with forty-degrees deflection, firing a long burst, and observed additional strikes and fire gushing from his right wing root and extending past the nacelle. I believe the pilot may have been wounded or killed either by my fire or that of Rosen's, because he lost control of his ship and crashed into an open field."

Rohrs was correct in his assumption—Feldwebel Heinz Wurm from 9 Staffel, JG 7, died in the crash of the Me 262.

Later that day, Lieutenants Mingo V. Logothetis and Claude G. Franklin, of the 12th Tactical Reconnaissance Squadron, were intercepted by an Me 262 during a visual recee mission of the Diekirch area. The jet made a firing pass at their section from six o'clock, but missed, and as the enemy craft pulled into a wing-over, Franklin fired at it. Logothetis then went after the 262, and in a series of diving turns, shot chunks from its wings, canopy and left engine. When he broke off combat, the jet's tail section was blazing. For some reason, Logothetis and Franklin were only credited with a probably destroyed from the encounter.

JANUARY 15, 1945

On January 15, marshalling yards in Germany were the targets, and Major Richard A. Peterson was leading the 364th Fighter Squadron, of the 357th Fighter Group. In the vicinity of Shongau, southwest of Munich, Peterson observed an airfield covered with planes and decided to take a few pictures with the K-25 camera that was installed on his aircraft. As the squadron orbited the field, Lieutenant Robert P. Winks noticed an aircraft performing a series of slow rolls down on the deck over the airfield and asked if he could go down after it. Peterson told him to go and down Winks went.

Winks dove from 15,000 feet, latched onto the tail of the bogie and fired a good burst just as it was approaching the airfield. Many strikes were observed and the fuselage burst into flames. The aircraft slammed into the edge of the field and blew up. Not until the gun camera film was viewed, did they identify the downed aircraft as an Me 262, which apparently had been putting on a show for the guys on the field when he was suddenly attacked.

JANUARY 20, 1945

The 357th Fighter Group again was assigned to escort bombers to their targets and did so without incident on January 20, then they proceeded to do some strafing. Lieutenant Dale E. Karger had been in on the strafing and had lost his flight leader in the action. As he looked up, he spied two Me 262s flying high above him. He and his wingman began a climb as the jets circled above them.

The Mustangs kept cutting the jets off as they attempted to come down, and finally one came at Karger almost head-on. As the 262 began a slow dive towards Munich, the jet pulled away from Karger, who thought he was going to lose it. At 5,000 feet, the jet made a long turn to the left, and Karger cut inside it. The Mustang pilot let go with one burst from long-range and saw a flash right in the cockpit. A few seconds later, the pilot bailed out, and the 262 split-essed and plummeted straight into the ground.

This marked the fifth victory for Karger, making him an ace at the age of nineteen. He was one of only three teenage aces in the U.S. Army Air Force during World War II.

Lieutenant Roland R. Wright, also of the 357th Fighter Group, successfully downed an Me 262 that day as well. He and his flight

Lieutenant Dale E. Karger was decorated for his feat of becoming an ace at 19 years of age, when he downed an Me 262 on January 20, 1944, over Lechfield airdrome. Karger flew a Mustang named Cathy Mae, *which is shown on the opposite page laden with drop tanks in preparation for an escort mission.* (Karger)

leader went after a jet that was attempting to land on Lechfeld airdrome. The two P-51s had turned across the edge of the field in order to fire on the enemy plane when his flight leader was hit by flak and forced to bail out.

Wright continued in, close to the deck, and opened fire. Immediately, the bullets from Wright's bevy of .50 calibers began to take their toll: The Me 262 ran off the runway and black smoke began rising high in the sky. Wright was forced to depart the area in a hurry, though, in order to avoid meeting the same fate as his flight leader.

Mid-January brought about the Luftwaffe's Revolt of the Aces when top German fighter aces Gunther Lutzow, Adolf Galland, Johannes Steinhoff and Hannes Trautloft met with Field Marshal Herman Goering to protest the use of the Messerschmitt Me 262s as bombers. They insisted that all production be turned over to fighter command. Goering stormed out of the meeting, and shortly thereafter, relieved all four of the Luftwaffe leaders of their assignments. Most important in the jet picture was the dismissal of Galland as commander of the German fighter forces. Galland was granted his wish when he was reassigned to command a new Luftwaffe unit flying Me 262s that would become known as JV 44.

THE MENACE GROWS

During the summer of 1944, several of the veteran bomber units of the Luftwaffe had been selected for conversion to fighters. Their pilots, who had logged many hours in Junkers Ju 88 and Heinkel He 111 bombers, were informed that they would be flying Me 109s, FW 190s and also Me 262s. One of the units initially selected for training in the Me 262 was 1/KG (J) 54. In November, the first jets began to arrive at their base at Giebelstadt. Group I flew its first formations during January 1945, when most of its pilots had logged about six hours in an Me 262.

FEBRUARY 9, 1945

The combat debut of 1/KG (J) 54 took place on February 9, 1945, when the Eighth Air Force attacked Fulda. Fifteen Me 262s from 1/KG (J) 54 rose to intercept them, but their initiation proved to be a disaster. Four of its aircraft were downed in the encounter, while two more were lost in crash landings. Among the pilots lost was the wing commander, Oberstleutnant Volprecht Riedesel Freiherr

Captain Don H. Bochkay, of the 357th Fighter Group, shot down an Me 262 on February 9, 1945, over Fulda, and he downed a second jet over Czechoslovakia on April 18, 1945. (Bochkay)

(Baron) zu Eisenbach, who collided in mid-air with Captain James W. Browning, a seven-victory ace from the 357th Fighter Group who was flying his second tour of combat.

Captain Donald H. Bochkay was flying Browning's wing that day and described the action: "At 1145 around the Fulda area, four Me 262s were called in by one of our flights, under us, at about 4,000 feet below, heading toward the bomber formation. We dropped our tanks, and Captain Browning dove to the left to attack. The four Me 262s broke up: Two dove to the right; two dove to the left. Browning never did get within range of the two going left and down. I climbed high, balls out, keeping the Me 262s in sight as well as covering Browning. I climbed to 28,000 feet and leveled off. Just as I leveled off, the two Me 262s broke right in a steep climbing turn. I called Browning and told him I was cutting them off.

"I dove my ship to gain more speed. The sun was in my favor, and I believe the Me 262s did not see me. I came in on the lead Me 262 but couldn't get my sights on him. I passed under the lead Me 262 and broke hard to the right, coming out on the second Me 262's tail at a very good range of 300 yards. I fired a long burst as he was pulling away from me, but I observed some very good hits about the canopy and right engine, which really slowed him down.

"The lead 262 headed straight down. The one I had hit broke to the left in a gentle turn, so I opened up on him again at about 400 yards and kept firing all the way in on him. I saw many strikes all over him, and his canopy shattered with large hunks flying off. I broke to the right to keep from running into him. As I passed very close to him, I saw the pilot halfway out of his cockpit. The ship rolled over on its back, and the pilot fell out. The pilot never opened his chute and the plane went straight in.

"I pulled up in a climbing left turn to rejoin Browning, but we got separated because there were so many P-51s in the area with the same colored tails. I found myself alone, so I set out to join up with someone in our own bunch. I saw another Me 262 diving and going like hell, followed by about seven P-51s, but out of range. I was

7,000 feet above them. The Me 262 then started to climb to the left, so I fire-walled it again and cut him off in a left turn, pulling my sight down on him at about a twenty-degree angle at 400 yards. I pulled the trigger, but only one gun fired, and six or seven rounds came out. I did not see any hits on him so I broke off, leaving him to someone else."

Lieutenant Johnnie L. Carter of the 357th Group was also credited with an Me 262 that day in the encounter with the former bomber pilots. Carter had to do a lot of chasing to get his victory. When his leader went after two Me 262s that split right from a formation of four, Carter went after the two that split left.

After ten to fifteen minutes of unsuccessfully pursuing these 262s, Carter sighted another jet 12,000 to 15,000 feet below him. The craft appeared to be throttled back and unaware of the Mustang above him. Carter split-essed and went down in a dive. This time, the P-51 closed rapidly. Carter opened fire and saw a few strikes. The Luftwaffe pilot didn't wait for anything else to happen, he bailed out.

An Me 262 fires up its engines and prepares to fly an interception. Some Me 262s were fitted with twelve R4M rockets under each wing. (via Ethell)

GERMAN JETS VS. THE U.S. ARMY AIR FORCE

Lieutenant Stephen Ananian of the 505th Fighter Squadron, of the 339th Fighter Group, was also in the Fulda area when he saw three Me 262s attack a bomber formation. One bomber went down and part of the crew bailed out. As Ananian closed on the jets, one of them made a pass at one of the parachutes that were floating down from the bomber. The pilot didn't fire—he may have been using his gun camera to confirm his victory. Ananian and a fellow pilot fired at the jet, but it was out of range, so Ananian tacked onto another jet that was coming towards him.

Ananian thought that he had the angle of interception worked out, but it didn't come out quite that way. He came out on the tail of the Me 262 all right, but at about 800 yards, which was rather a long range for his guns.

However, he fired a three-second burst and was surprised to notice strikes along the wings and left engine of the enemy aircraft. The pilot attempted to speed away from the Mustang, but apparently he had been hit in the left engine, for his throttling sent him veering sharply to the left.

Ananian had now closed the gap to about 600 yards, so he fired another three-second burst, placing strikes on the canopy and engine nacelles. As the jet dove, the Mustang pilot fired again. The left engine began to smoke, and the right engine suddenly ignited. The Me 262 continued downward, out of control, the pilot did not get out.

A bit later, in the vicinity of Meiningen, Lieutenant Jerome J. Sainlar saw an Me 262 attacking two B-17s that had dropped out of formation. The Mustangs of the 504th Fighter Squadron went to the rescue, and Sainlar managed to get the best cutoff, registering hits from forty-degrees deflection. The Me 262 left the area in a dive. Sainlar only claimed a damaged in that combat, but John Foreman in his book, *Me 262 Combat Diary*, states that Sainlar actually shot down the aircraft piloted by Unteroffizier Heinz Speck of 3/EJG 2, who was killed in the crash.

February 15, 1945

On February 15, oil was once more the target, and a recovering 1/JG (J) 54 put Me 262s in the air to intercept the mission. Apparently, however, they did not down any of the bombers. Lieutenant Dudley M. Amoss of the 55th Fighter Group was flying down low, at only 2,000 feet, when he sighted a 262 at 1,000 feet below.

The Luftwaffe pilot was apparently caught off guard for he didn't throttle forward until he was under attack. Amoss came in on his tail and opened fire with a long burst. The jet pilot immediately tried to speed away, but he was hit in his engines. Amoss then closed to 200 yards and fired a number of short bursts, prompting an explosion as the 262 burst into flames. The pilot finally got out at about 500 feet.

February 21, 1945

A few skirmishes occurred here and there, in which neither the jets, nor the American fighters, were able to down any planes. The next victorious combat came on February 21, while an American fighter was escorting a photo reconnaissance pilot. Lieutenant Harold E. Whitmore and Lieutenant Russell N. Webb were assigned to accompany an F-5 reconnaissance aircraft on its mission to the port of Stettin and back.

At 1530 hours, the three aircraft were over Stettin. The F-5 pilot flew at 20,000 feet, taking his pictures, and Whitmore was up at 22,000 feet, above and to the right of the F-5. Webb flew at 21,000 feet, to the left of the recee craft. Whitmore spotted an Me 262 coming up from the rear at high speed. He quickly called the photo plane and told the pilot: "Break, there is a jet coming up your ass."

The recee pilot didn't break, however, he just dipped his left wing. Whitmore chopped throttle, left his tanks on and pushed his nose over, making his bounce. He came in from five o'clock high as the jet opened fire on the F-5. Just as Whitmore was ready to open fire, though, the jet turned to the left and down. The jet had hit the F-5—its right engine was ablaze.

When Whitmore had called in the jet, Webb had dropped his tanks, chopped throttle and slid high to the outside. When the Me 262 made his left turn and went down after hitting the F-5, it passed directly in front of Webb's nose. Webb fired, but did not get any strikes. Whitmore then fired from about 300 yards right on the jet's tail, scoring a number of hits on the wing and fuselage.

Webb fell in trail of Whitmore, who continued to close and fire on the Me 262. A long burst from 400 yards set the aircraft afire, and it began to disintegrate. The pilot of this aircraft was probably Oberfahnrich Gerhard Ronde of 2/KG (J) 51.

Following the destruction of the Me 262, Whitmore and Webb searched for the F-5, but they never sighted the aircraft again. On the way home, they spotted another Me 262 below, and both Mustang pilots went down. The jet, however, split-essed and escaped.

FEBRUARY 22, 1945

February 22, 1945, marked the day of Operation Clarion, during which all Allied aircraft were involved in assaults on German rail and road communications. All bomb groups participated, and the jets arose to challenge them, engaging in several sharp actions, though bomber losses were minimal.

3/JG 7 put up thirty-four Me 262s to challenge the bomber stream. In the vicinity of Stendal, four of the jets were intercepted by the 352nd Fighter Group in their blue-nosed Mustangs, but not before the Germans had shot down two of the bombers. Major Earl Duncan managed to cut off the attack of one of the jets and forced it to zoom up into the territory of the 486th Fighter Squadron. There Lieutenant Charles Goodman managed to damage the right engine with a well-placed burst.

Immediately after Duncan had sent one jet climbing upstairs, he encountered another. Duncan went after it and managed to get some strikes, which drew forth a stream of black smoke, but the Mustang pilot was cut off by another flight of P-51s.

Lieutenant Charles D. Price of the 486th Fighter Squadron had dropped his tanks and followed his flight leader down after a 262 that was stalking a B-17. Price was flying behind and high to his flight leader. Price recalled: "The Me 262 chandelled off the bomber box and cut in front of me. I broke after him and started firing at 400 yards.

"Observed strikes on his wings and knocked off a few fragments. I continued firing and then saw several large chunks fall off when one of the jet engines started smoking. He fell off into a tight spiral, going down, and I followed through, rolling with him. I continued firing on the way down until the whole fuselage burst into flame and exploded."

Major Wayne Blickenstaff led the 353rd Fighter Group on a fighter sweep in the Berlin area, where they sighted and chased a number of Me 262s. The Mustangs first met four of the jets in the vicinity of Brandenburg, but when they attempted to engage, the 262s broke up and led the P-51s on a merry chase over Berlin. The craft that Blickenstaff went after headed to the east, and finally, the Mustang leader gave it up, as he knew he was approaching the Russian lines.

The 353rd fighters headed back northwest of Berlin and were flying at 8,000 feet, when Blickenstaff noted another 262 flying east, down in the haze. He split-essed and managed to close on the jet before his presence was known. At 600 yards, he opened fire and got strikes on the left jet engine, which began to stream white smoke. The 262 pilot began to take wild evasive action, and Blickenstaff could not keep his sights on him. The Luftwaffe pilot then headed for the deck as Blickenstaff fired again and began to score more hits on the left jet engine. The pilot jettisoned his canopy and bailed out.

Captain Gordon B. Compton had been leading the 351st Fighter Squadron, of the 353rd Group, behind Blickenstaff when he sighted the bogies. Blickenstaff had gone into a left turn after the first four Me 262s, so Compton, some miles behind, went into a left turn to cut the jets off.

He later related: "I first picked up the bogies flying string forma-tion and in a diving left turn. There were four of them—Me 262s. I started after the No. 3 man, but he was too far away, and I was unable to close. So, I waited for the No. 4 man to pull out. He did and turned right in front of me. I did not have time to track and range with my K-14 sight, so I picked out his line of flight and fired a long burst for him to fly through. I saw a few strikes on the right jet unit, and it began to trail white smoke.

"With the unit crippled, the Me 262 was unable to pull away, and I got dead astern of him, firing at about 350 yards. Hunks flew off following one burst, and finally, he pulled up sharply to the left, climbing several thousand feet per minute. Then the right jet unit burst into flames, and the pilot rolled over and bailed out."

The 364th Fighter Group was escorting bombers to Wittstock, when they were hit by a formation of twelve-plus Me 262s. Lieu-tenant Francis Radley was shot down by one of the jets on the initial bounce. As the fighters began to mix it up, Captain Richard W. Stevens (the victor over Major Nowotny) and his wingman, Lieu-tenant Clarence B. Kirby, went after a pair of Me 262s. One partner went into a turn to get on their tails, but they disregarded this and continued after their prey.

Stevens recalled the combat, which involved some smart maneu-vering by the Luftwaffe pilots: "We slowly closed range at over 400 IAS and in a slight dive to the east. I opened fire with a short burst at 600 yards and dead astern of the lead jet, while my No. 2 man chased the other. The jets seemed to work together, because when I opened fire on one, the other attempted to get behind me. But my wingman chased him away. I continued to fire short bursts, seeing some smoke and strikes, but was unable to close to less than about 600 yards. Both E/A led us to an airfield, where they seemed to be trying to land. The jet I fired on made a 180-degree turn around the field, then I was forced to break off the attack by a third Me 262 that had been flying over the field. I attempted to make an attack on the newcomer, but I had only one gun left and observed no strikes.

"My No. 2 man had to break away from original attack by a jet on his tail, but was able to force home an attack on the 262 that I had damaged. He made two passes on this E/A before being forced to withdraw by another jet. I was too far away to observe damage, but I saw the first Me 262 in a slight dive at 1,000 feet, with its wheels down, about five miles from the airfield. It was going from side-to-side, apparently out of control. It must have crash landed, but we couldn't wait around to see. I was out of ammunition, running out of gas and other jets were around. I called to Kirby to come along and we set course for home."

The first three losses by 3/JG 7 for the day were observed and con-firmed, which would cover the victories of Price, Blickenstaff and Compton. The fourth loss by 3/JG 7 that day was an Me 262 that was forced to crash land and assessed as 80 percent destroyed, would fit the picture of the Me 262 Stevens and Kirby had worked over.

That afternoon, Captain Charles Ready, Jr., of the

Captain Gordon B. Compton of the 353rd Fighter Group, downed an Me 262 during an escort mission in the Berlin area on February 22, 1945. Compton scored his second Me 262 victory on April 10, 1945, in the Dessau area. (Compton)

388th Fighter Squadron, 365th Fighter Group, Ninth Air Force, led a force of nine Thunderbolts out on an armed reconnaissance mission. At 1730 hours, their ground control reported that four Me 262s were strafing roads behind Allied lines on the Pier-Duren highway. The P-47s were already in the area and soon sighted one of the Me 262s. Red Flight, with Ready leading, went down after it, and they pursued it off to the east towards Germany.

Lieutenant Oliver T. Cowan was leading White Flight up at 11,000 feet when the jet was sighted, and he saw the 262 pulling away from Red Flight. As the Luftwaffe pilot was leaving Red Flight behind, Cowan and his wingman, Lieutenant Thomas Threlkeld, split-essed and went down after him. The Thunderbolts were going balls-out, and at 5,000 feet, Cowan noted that he was doing more than 500 MPH. The 262 pilot did not see the P-47 until it was too late. Cowan shallowed his dive, pulled the nose through and opened fire. The eight .50-caliber guns took their toll. Cowan lost sight of

Ninth Air Force P-47 Thunderbolt pilot Lieutenant Oliver T. Cowan shot down a KG 51 Me 262 that was attacking American troops in the Duren area on February 22, 1945. (USAAF)

THE MENACE GROWS

the 262 down at 300 feet, but when he lowered his nose to fire again, he saw the Me 262 smack into the ground.

The 366th Fighter Group, of the Ninth Air Force, was flying its second mission of the day when one of its pilots encountered and downed an Arado 234. Lieutenant David B. Fox reported: "I was flying Red Three in the 391st Squadron formation led by Major Brinson. On our way home from a dive bombing mission, I spotted a lone Ar 234 and used water to catch him.

I dove on him, closing fast, began shooting about fifty to sixty degrees until I was in trail, when I ran out of ammunition. I observed strikes all over the plane. One large portion flew off, probably the canopy, and a fire started in the right engine. The plane went down smoking, and I followed it to the deck. Our own flak became so intense that we had to break off our pursuit. The planes continued a bit farther and finally bellied in."

February 25, 1945

February 25, 1945, proved to be a busy and black day for the German jets. Twice they were in action en mass, and both times it cost them, once severely. Thunderbolts of the 386th Fighter Squadron, 365th Fighter Group, of the Ninth Air Force, were out early on that bright and clear day. Each P-47 was laden with two 500-pound bombs or with napalm bombs. The squadron was led by Lieutenant John H. Rogers and the eight aircraft rendezvoused over Duren, Germany, where they were vectored bombs on targets at Morschenich. There they hit the town that was holding up the advance of the 104th U.S. Infantry Division. Following that mission, they went after a marshalling yard at Elsdorf, where they strafed the yard and attacked a locomotive.

Ground control contacted the squadron and informed them that jet enemy aircraft were in the Duren area. The Thunderbolts headed for the area immediately, and on arrival they found fifteen Me 262s, which no doubt belonged to 1/JG (J) 51 from bases at Rheine and Hopsten. As soon as the jets saw the P-47s, they headed west.

During this engagement, Lieutenant Alfred Longo experienced engine trouble and was sent home. However, en route, as he crossed the Roer River, he was attacked by an Me 262 that was blazing away. Longo broke left, pulling as many Gs as he could and found that he easily outturned the jet. He fired a long burst before his P-47 stalled out and saw pieces fly off the 262, then it pulled straight up and headed for a patch of clouds.

Lieutenant James L. McWhorter had climbed up to 4,000 feet following the jet sighting when he saw two Me 262s closing on his tail from about 8,000 feet. He immediately turned into them and fired as the jets came at him head-on.

He registered a few strikes, but when McWhorter completed his 180-degree turn, the jets were long gone. McWhorter climbed up to 12,000 feet where he saw an Me 262 making a pass at one of his flights. The Thunderbolt pilot opened fire from long-range, spewing plenty of lead. Black smoke began to belch from the jet, but it broke sharply to the north, and McWhorter was unable to pursue.

Many of the Eighth Air Force fighters had been turned loose to locate and attack the Luftwaffe bases that housed the jets. Which is exactly what the 55th Fighter Group did with great success. They arrived over Giebelstadt airdrome just as the ill-fated 1/JG (J) 54 was getting airborne.

Captain Donald E. Penn, who was leading the 55th Group reported: "… I noticed two Me 262s airborne and two more taking off from Giebelstadt airdrome. We were flying at 13,000 feet, and I ordered the squadron to drop tanks and engage the E/A. I dived on one jet, using fifty inches of mercury and 3,000 RPM.

"He was making a slight turn to port at 1,000 feet, heading back toward the drome, so I leveled off 3,000 yards behind him and went to full power. My IAS was about 500 MPH, and I expected him to use full-power as well to attempt to pull away from me. However, I closed rapidly, firing from 1,000 yards."

"At 500 yards, I observed the 262 had his wheels down. I cut down on my power, and at 300 yards started striking the aircraft in the power unit. Closing to 50 yards, I broke sharply over the top of the jet, watching him as he rolled over, went straight in and exploded."

Also in the air during the attack on Giebelstadt, Lieutenant John F. O'Neil descended and immediately lined up on an Me 262 with its wheels down. Closing fast, the Mustang pilot gave him a long five-second burst and observed multiple strikes. As O'Neil pulled up, he saw the left engine erupt into flames. Captain Frank E. Birtciel fired at the aircraft, too, just before it crashed and exploded. Birtciel did not claim the aircraft.

Captain Donald M. Cummings was leading Hellcat Yellow Flight when Penn called for the attack, so he dropped his tanks and descended to the jet airdrome. As one of the Me 262s approached the field, Cummings latched onto its tail and opened fire from 1,000 yards in a steep diving pass.

Many strikes were seen, and Cummings continued to close. By now, however, heavy flak was erupting from the airdrome, and Cummings was forced to pull up. His wingman, who was just behind him, saw the jet touch ground, cartwheel and burn.

Cummings pulled up from the field to 5,000 feet and set out to find further targets. Near Leipheim airdrome, he spotted a bogie down at 4,000 feet, crossing below. Cummings dropped down in a shallow dive and increased his speed to close on the aircraft. As soon as he identified the bogie as an Me 262, the enemy aircraft went turned to the left and continued letting down, apparently in an attempt to land. Cummings closed to 400 yards and opened fire. The first burst missed, but when the jet went into a turn to the right, the Mustang pilot fired again, and large chunks of the aircraft began to peel off. Suddenly, the jet's fuselage exploded, and the 262 rolled over and plunged into the deck from 800 feet.

Lieutenant Billy Clemmons had followed Penn down, but he and his wingman were on the inside of the turn, so they circled the field while the first three jets were destroyed. Clemmons and his wingman then climbed to clear the surroundings, when an Me 262 was seen flying west at about 1,000 feet. Clemmons was at 3,000 feet, heading east, and he made a diving turn to come in behind the jet. The German pilot saw him and pulled his 262 up in a steep chandelle to the right, but the P-51 stayed right with it. However, the enemy pilot must have thought he had lost Clemmons for he leveled off.

The P-51 pilot then pulled up to 300 yards and hit the 262 with a three-second burst that blasted holes in the left jet engine and the canopy. The enemy pilot began to climb to the left, trying to escape, but Clemmons hit the jet twice more, getting continual hits. The jet continued to climb and take hits until it reached 5,000 feet. Then, it rolled over on its back and went into a spin that continued all the way down to earth. There was no parachute.

Lieutenant Millard O. Anderson was leading the second element of Hellcat Yellow Flight during the Geibelstadt massacre, but when he approached the field, all the jets were either downed or being chased. Anderson went after two FW 190s that were trying to land. He came down right on their tails and opened fire on the aircraft on the right. He strafed it all the way down the runway but had to pull up due to the flak streaming up at him. His wingman, behind him, told him that the FW 190 had been burning on the runway when he had crossed over it.

Anderson climbed back up to 5,500 feet, where he spied an Me 262 at his ten o'clock and 3,000 feet below. He quickly did a wing-over and closed on the jet from dead astern. Anderson's gun sight was out, so he just centered the 262 in the middle of his windshield, opened fire and held it until he saw hits. The 262 flamed and its wheels dropped. The pilot went over the side and popped his parachute.

The last claimant for the 55th that day was Lieutenant Donald T. Menegay, Anderson's wingman. The two had been separated after Anderson's pass on the FW 190 and he had lost his R/T connection at the same time. Menegay went alone at 6,000 feet and noticed a

262 flying below, at 4,000 feet. He went into a steep turn and brought his Mustang in on the tail of the jet from about 1,500 yards. Menegay opened fire, closing to 1,000 yards but saw no hits. He held the pipper of his sight on the 262 and fired all his ammunition. Slowly, hits began to register on the Me 262 and smoke roiled from the left engine. The pilot then bailed out, and just as he fell clear of the aircraft, it exploded.

Against the American claims of seven jets destroyed, it is known that 1I and 2/JG (J) 54 lost six Me 262s on February 25. The pilots killed were Leutenants Hans-Georg Knobel and Josef Lackner; Feldwebels Heinz Clausner and Felix Einhardt, and Leutenant Wolf Zimmermann had bailed out, all wounded; and another 262 crash landed on the airfield. Later in the day, four of the unit's Me 262s were destroyed on the ground during strafing attacks, and two more were lost to accident.

It was a day from which the unit never recovered.

On February 25, the 4th Fighter Group was also out strafing. Lieutenant Carl G. Payne of the 334th Fighter Squadron was flying Comweb Blue 3 that morning. The Mustangs were ten minutes southwest of Leipzig at 8,000 feet, when Payne saw an Me 262 flying at 4,000 feet, at one o'clock. Payne described the encounter: "I peeled off on him, calling in at the same time. I closed to about 400 yards and opened fire, holding it until about 100 yards. I hit him and knocked out his left jet engine. I overshot him and pulled up to the right to make another pass. During the pass, I was not striking him as I should, so I moved up to ten to thirty feet behind him and started firing again; the jet exploded, covering me completely with flames."

Some pilots say pulling up so close to an enemy aircraft and firing was a good way to destroy yourself, while others believe the pilot should pull up until the aircraft completely covers your windshield.

Two pilots from the 385th Fighter Squadron, of the 364th Fighter Group, happened up on an Arado 234 in the Steinhuder Lake area at about eleven o'clock that morning. Lieutenant Eugene Murphy said: "The jet was at 2,000 feet and I was at 5,000. He started a medium turn to the left, and I overhauled him at about ninety degrees of his turn. I opened fire at 800 yards, firing a long burst to catch him before he gave it the gun.

"At about 180 degrees in his turn, I put a burst into his left engine and a long burst along his wings and into his fuselage. I ended up dead astern when my ammo gave out. The jet leveled out as if to land. I was doing about 350 MPH at the time. I pulled up to cover my No. 4 man, who took over and saw the jet crash and burn."

No. 4 man, Lieutenant Richard E. White, stated: "I made a slight turn to the left to get on the jet's tail when he cut all his power. I chopped my power, but still overtook him. I passed about fifty yards behind him, and I fired a burst as I crossed his tail. I ended up practically flying in formation on his left wing, about thirty feet away, with my power cut and forty-degree flaps. The pilot looked at me and tried to turn to the right, but instead he did a half-roll about thirty feet above the ground and slammed into the ground upside down, exploding in a ball of flames."

While the jet units were still having their problems, particularly the KG units with former bomber pilots flying the Me 262s, the interceptor units, or JG units, were building up. JG 7 was receiving more aircraft all the time, despite the fact that many of the new jets were being destroyed during aerial bombardments of manufacturing facilities and during ground strafing and bombings of the airfields. More young jet fighter pilots were being trained and sent to JG 7 for further instruction from veteran combat pilots.

During February, General Adolf Galland formed the new JV 44 unit, which was manned largely by top-scoring Luftwaffe aces. Some sources said that, early in the organization's history, entry into the elite unit required the Knights Cross. American bomber crews would feel the force of these fighter units during the remaining months of World War II in Europe. American fighter pilots were forced to rely on all their devices to trap the enemy jets and prevent decimation of their bomber formations.

CHAPTER 4

THE MENACE BECOMES A PROBLEM

B ombers from Eighth Air Force set out to bomb marshalling yards on March 1, but nasty weather conditions prevented a few of them from attacking their assigned targets. The 355th Fighter Group was escorting B-24 bombers to Ingelstadt, Germany. Flying with the Bentley Flight, of the 358th Fighter Squadron, was Lieutenant Wendell W. Beaty. The B-24s had collected at the Initial Point before turning on the bomb run at 19,000 feet. Beaty and his Mustangs were flying at 22,000, behind the bombers, when an Me 262 approached the bombers from 23,000 feet. By the time the P-51s could react, though, the jet was long gone.

A minute later, another Me 262 came in directly toward the Mustangs from one o'clock. The P-51 pilots immediately went after it, and the jet pilot went into a right-hand turn. As the Mustangs went down after it, the jet joined a flight of four more Me 262s. The P-51 pilots went into maneuvers to cut the jets off, but some of them rolled out and pulled away in a blaze of speed.

Beaty was going after one of the jets in a dive, when another flew directly in front of him from nine o'clock. Beaty swiftly rolled out and flew in pursuit of the 262 from dead astern, at 15,000 feet. Beaty opened fire from 600 yards and hit the left wing near the engine nacelle. The jet pilot kicked his bird in the rear, just as Beaty hit him with another long burst.

Once more, a Luftwaffe jet pilot made the fatal mistake of turning. Beaty cut him off, and when the 262 pilot reversed his turn to the left, the Mustang pilot turned inside him again. The jet then dove down after a cloud layer at 6,000 feet, which was only 1,500 to 2,000 feet deep. Beaty followed him down in a steep dive, speeding faster than 500 MPH. Just as the P-51 pilot broke out of the clouds, he and his wingman saw the jet crash and explode.

Meanwhile, Lieutenant John K. Wilkins, Jr., of the 2nd Scouting Force, which was attached to the 355th Fighter Group, engaged and shot down another of the Me 262s out of the same formation that Beaty had intercepted. Major Frank Elliott, of the 2nd Scouting Force, also managed to damage one of the jets from that formation. The downed jets were from 1/KG (J) 54, and the two German pilots who were shot down were both killed.

As the American pilots mixed it up more and more with the Me 262s, it was quite obvious that they just did not obtain the same intensity of explosions from destroying the jets that they received from the conventional Luftwaffe fighters. The low-grade jet fuel didn't ignite and explode in the manner that the customary gasoline did. This had already inspired ordinance to see if they could come up with a more incendiary ammunition. Some effort was expended on this project.

MARCH 2, 1945

The pilots of KG (J) 51 were becoming more proficient with their jets all the time, and they illustrated a bit of their prowess against the 365th Fighter Group on March 2. On four different occasions, the jets attacked flights of four Thunderbolts while they were on dive bombing assignments. Once, they managed to make their passes before the P-47s were over their target, which forced them to drop their bombs to engage the enemy. However, the jets raced away at full-throttle, leaving their unhappy pursuers far behind.

That morning, P-51s of the 354th Fighter Group mixed it up with Me 262s from 1/KG (J) 54. Captain Bruno Peters of the 355th Fighter Squadron led a fighter sweep to Fulda, and south to Kassel, where two Me 262s were shot down over the enemy's airdrome. Diving from 12,000 feet through haze and overcast, Peters caught the first jet at 1,500 feet. Flight Officer Ralph Delgado pursued, scoring many strikes on the second jet, and the pilot bailed out. Apparently, no one saw Peter's victim go in, for it was officially credited as destroyed unconfirmed. However, 1/KG (J) 54 lost Feldwebel Heinrich Griem, and Feldwebel Gunther Gorlitz bailed out.

THE MENACE BECOMES A PROBLEM

Later that same morning, Lieutenant Theodore W. Sedvert, of the 353rd Fighter Squadron, jumped an Me 262 south of Dilligen and shot it down.

While on a morning reconnaissance mission, Lieutenant Floyd T. Dunmire, flying an F-6 from the 107th Reconnaissance Squadron, of the 67th Reconnaissance Group, combatted an Me 262 from 5/JG (J) 51 flown by Hauptman Fritz Abel. Contact was made near Koln, and Abel was shot down and killed near Nijmegen.

MARCH 3, 1945

On March 3, 3/JG 7 put up twenty-six Me 262s to intercept bombers that were attacking oil refineries in central Germany. The initial jet attacks were against B-17s in the Magdeburg area, and later B-24s came under attack in the same area. Nine Eighth Air Force bombers were lost that day, and some of them undoubtedly fell to jets. However, it is known that Hauptmann Guttman from 9 Staffel of JG 7 was shot down and killed by fire from a B-17 formation.

Six claims were made by Mustang pilots on Me 262s during the day, but all were credited as damaged.

In mid-March, through a hard-fought battle, the Allies took the Ludendorff Railroad Bridge across the Rhine River at Remagen—a momentous occurrence in their favor. For nine consecutive days, KG 76 had used Arado 234 jet bombers in attempts to destroy the bridge.

MARCH 13, 1945

Further sharp action between units of the U.S. Army Air Force and the German jets did not occur until the morning of March 13, when Thunderbolts from the 388th Fighter Squadron, of the 365th Fighter Group, encountered four Me 262s flying at 16,000 feet northeast of Cologne. Lieutenant Archie F. Maltbie, leading the squadron of twelve P-47s, called them in to his White and Blue Flights, which were cruising at 20,000 feet.

Lieutenant Frederick W. Marling, who was flying Blue Three, along with Lieutenant Henry Dahlen, Blue Four, joined in the chase after the jets, which soon outdistanced them. Maltbie called the chase off, and the Thunderbolt pilots began to climb to re-form. As Marling and Dahlen reached 17,000 feet, Marling sighted an Me 262 heading east at 7,000 feet.

The two Thunderbolt pilots split-essed and went down on the tail of the unsuspecting jet pilot. Marling began to fire at 300 to 400 yards and closed to 200 yards, getting good strikes all the way.

Suddenly, an explosion caused gray smoke to belch from the fuselage of the 262. The plane headed down toward the clouds, trailing gray smoke. Marling's right-wing guns had ceased firing, so he called to Dahlen to take over. Before Dahlen could position his Thunderbolt, however, the jet slipped into some clouds at 4,000 feet and vanished. It seems that Marling downed one of the two KG (J) 51 jets that were lost that day.

Captain Donald S. Bryan attacked and shot down an Arado 234 in the vicinity of Efstaffthal on March 14, 1945. (Bryan)

THE MENACE BECOMES A PROBLEM

On March 14, several Arado 234 bombers and Me 262s made attempts to bomb the bridge at Remagen. The first encounter was with the 352nd Fighter Group, when their Mustangs were withdrawing from a mission on which they had provided escort for Ninth Air Force bombers. Captain Donald S. Bryan sighted an Arado heading for the bridge, as the jet crossed south of the Rhine River, heading west, then turned north to make a shallow run on the bridge. However, Bryan saw no bombs drop.

Bryan could not catch the jet, but he spotted P-47s coming in from the northeast and hoped that their presence might caught the Arado to turn. Sure enough, the Luftwaffe pilot saw them, too, and turned east. This turn led the Ar 234 under Bryan, who dove down on it. The Mustang pilot opened fire from 250 yards and knocked out the right jet engine with his first burst.

The jet pilot went into a shallow turn and performed some gentle evasive maneuvers, which did not really interfere with Bryan's firing. Both engines were knocked out, and the enemy craft was emitting clouds of white smoke. The Arado slipped over on its back and went down in a steep diving crash.

Lieutenant Sanborn N. Ball, Jr., was leading a flight of P-47s from the 62nd Fighter Squadron in the Coblenz area, when a flight of three Arado Ar 234 bombers crossed under him. Ball was not aware that they were enemy planes until he got a good look at them below. Ball and his flight dropped their tanks and went down after them. Ball's element leader, Lieutenant Warren S. Lear, latched onto the tail of an Arado and set its left engine smoking before he overran the plane. Ball then closed, opened fire from 500 yards and continued to fire until he overran the jet. The German pilot jettisoned his canopy and bailed out just as Lear made his second pass. The aircraft, leaderless, fell into a downward spiral.

Lieutenant Norman D. Gould of the 62nd Squadron then arrived on the scene. He immediately attacked one of the 234s from astern and clobbered it. The right engine of the jet burst into flames, and the aircraft went into a spin from which it did not recover.

Lieutenant Robert E. Barnhart, of the 356th Fighter Group, was on his way out of Germany after escorting the bombers, when he noticed an aircraft heading into Germany and decided to go after it. After a futile ten- to fifteen-minute chase, Barnhart was about ready to give up, when the bogie made a left turn to the north.

As Barnhart reported it: "Unable to identify it, I closed until I saws the jets and the German markings. Feeling that I had him cold, I slid under him and came up on his right, about thirty feet from him, in order to get a good look at this plane. I could not identify it then, but have since recognized it from drawings as the Arado 234.

"The pilot of the jet looked over at me, immediately jettisoned his canopy and bailed out. After he had bailed, the plane continued flying in a wide right orbit. Obviously, its power was still on, as it circled for more than ten minutes, holding its altitude. I made a pass, taking a short picture of the aircraft, and then photographed the pilot in his chute."

After taking more photos, Barnhart decided to fly firing passes at the 234, using it for target practice until it flamed and spun down.

The final jet victory of the day was scored by Lieutenant Charles R. Rodebaugh, of the 2nd Scouting Force. He was leading his flight in the Coblenz area, when he saw an Me 262 flying 10,000 feet below him. Rodebaugh split-essed and went down after the jet. The Luftwaffe pilot sighted the Mustang, and instead of throttling away, he dropped his bomb and went into a right turn.

This enabled the American pilot to turn inside him and open fire from 700 yards. Strikes appeared around the cockpit and right wing. Rodebaugh noted that the plane suddenly seemed to be out of control. The 262 slowly rolled over and dove straight for the ground. The pilot did not attempt to bail out.

THE MENACE BECOMES A PROBLEM

The Eighth Air Force sent its bombers to Zossen an Oranienburg on March 15. Despite limited interceptions, Me 262s from JG 7 made several claims. The only American jet victory was scored by Captain Ray. S. Wetmore of the 359th Fighter Group who downed an Me 163 near Wittenberg.

Wetmore reported: "… southwest of Berlin I saw two Me 163s circling at about 20,000 feet, twenty miles away in the vicinity of Wittenberg. I flew over towards them, and while at 25,000 feet, started after one a little below me. When I got within 3,000 yards, he saw me, turned on his jet and went up in a seventy-degree climb.

At about 26,000 feet, his jet quit, and he split-essed. I dove with him and leveled off at 2,000 feet, on him at six o'clock. During the dive, my IAS was between 550 and 600 MPH. I opened fire at 200

Captain Ray S. Wetmore was credited with the last victory over an Me 163 in the Wiffenberg area on March 15, 1945. (USAAF)

GERMAN JETS VS. THE U.S. ARMY AIR FORCE

yards. Pieces flew off all over. He made a sharp turn to the right, and I gave him another short burst. About half his left wing flew off, and the plane caught fire. The pilot bailed out, and I saw the craft crash into the ground."

That day, American pilots sighted several Me 163s. This would prove to be the last 163 encounters of any size. Apparently, none of the rocket-powered pilots were very successful.

MARCH 17, 1945

The 8th Bomber Command was out in force on March 17, but fighter combat was quite limited. Heavy clouds covered the target areas, and only a few Me 262s put in an appearance to oppose them. The Luftwaffe jets claimed four bombers, and it is possible that some of the five Me 262s lost may have fallen to them. Only one American pilot claimed as much as a damaged against the Luftwaffe jets that day.

MARCH 18, 1945

While no Luftwaffe jets were downed by American fighters on March 18, the German jets put up their most effective defense against bombers of the Eighth Air Force to date. The Americans launched a massive strike, composed of 1,329 heavy bombers, against railway stations and tank plants in the Berlin area.

The Eighth Air Force Intelligence Operational Summary for the day stated: "A combination of well-coordinated and aggressive jet attacks, plus cloud and contrail conditions that favored enemy tactics and hindered escort, resulted in a limited though noteworthy success for German Air Force jet interceptors. The loss of at least six bombers is attributed to enemy aircraft action.

"The First Force (450 B-17s of the 1st Air Division) reported losing two bombers to attacks by some fifteen to twenty Me 262s from approximately 1110 to 1130 in the target area. ... The enemy aircraft used contrails from which to launch attacks that were aggressively pressed home against the last two groups, in one instance, to as close as fifty yards. … Jet enemy aircraft skillfully used their superior speed and although escorting fighters engaged the enemy aircraft they succeeded in damaging only one of them.

"The Second Force (530 B-17s of the 3rd Air Division) was strongly attacked by some twelve to fifteen Me 262s, from 1105 to 1130 hours, in the area extending from just west of Salzwedel to Berlin. Enemy attacks, though not continuous, were aggressive and skillful. Contrail cover was effectively used, and four bombers went down to the enemy jets. Weather conditions aggravated the escort problem; bomber crews reported they were unable to contact their escorts during the attacks.

The first attack came some twenty minutes before target when the enemy singled out the low squadron of the second group in the column. This squadron, at the time, was strung out and in poor formation. Four Me 262s in a formation similar to that used by our P-51s, came out of the clouds and bomber contrails from five o'clock low, closing from seventy yards to almost point-blank range, to badly damage three bombers on the first pass. A second attack, made by three Me 262s from six-thirty to seven o'clock low to level, resulted in the entire tail section of one of the B-17s being shot off.

"… Today's concerted attacks by jet enemy aircraft, small scale though they were, indicate progress by the German Air Force in developing tactics to bring down heavy bombers. Coordinated attacks by formations of three to four jet enemy aircraft will probably continue. And as enemy jet strength increases and operational experience accrues, larger mass attacks may be attempted.

"A touch of the old Hun cunning and aggressive spirit was apparent today in the advantage taken of cloud and contrail cover for launching attacks and in directing his attention to a vulnerable, strung-out formation."

Leading the attack against the First Force was Major Theodor Weissenberger, Kommodore of JG 7 and a famed Luftwaffe ace with

200 victories to his credit. Weissenberger claimed victories over two B-17s in this attack. This formation suffered two losses to the jets, and another ten aircraft landed in Soviet-occupied territory after suffering extensive battle damage during the course of the mission.

One of the B-17s lost by the 1st Air Division was from the 457th Bomb Group. This aircraft, flown by Lieutenant John W. Schwikert, was badly damaged by one of the jets but continued to fly in its position until its No. 2 engine caught on fire, and the crew was forced to bail out.

Some of the jet attackers flying against the 3rd Air Division were outfitted with new R4M rockets. The 55 MM rocket contained a potent explosive that was capable of inflicting heavy destruction. The rockets were carried in batteries of twelve, which were mounted in wooden racks carried outboard of the engine nacelles. These rockets, coupled with the 30 MM cannon in the nose, gave the Me 262 the most lethal armament of any fighter plane in the air over Europe.

Feldwebel Rolf Glogner is shown preparing for a flight in an Me 163. Note the conventional ladder that was used to mount the wing. (via Ethell)

THE MENACE BECOMES A PROBLEM

The "strung-out" squadron that had been caught by the German jet force was the low squadron of the 100th Bomb Group. First hit was *Skyway Chariot,* flown by Lieutenant Rollie King. In its initial pass, an Me 262 shot the *Chariot's* left stabilizer off, and the aircraft started down. In the second attack, that B-17 was spun violently as it took two more direct hits under the flight deck and into the root of the right wing. The pilot gave the order to jump, and the aircraft blew up as the crew departed.

Six of the nine men aboard successfully bailed out and were taken as prisoners of war. The ball turret, waist and tail gunners were killed in the attacks.

Sweet Nancy, flown by Lieutenant Edward Gwin, was hit by an Me 262 and dove away with two engines afire. The aircraft then nosed up, and its tail fell off and went down spinning. Six of the crew bailed out and survived.

The lead ship, flown by Lieutenant Paul DeWeerdt, with the command pilot, Captain Roger Swain aboard, was hit in the left wing, destroying the aircraft's No. 1 engine. The fuel tanks then ignited, forcing the crew to bail out. All escaped the craft except the engineer gunner, who refused to bail out. DeWeerdt evaded capture and made his way to Allied lines, while the rest of the crew were taken prisoner.

The fourth Fortress in the squadron that had been hit was flown by Lieutenant Merrill Jensen. The navigator, Lieutenant Richard Scroxton, reported that there was no warning of enemy aircraft until four Me 262s came at their tail out of the contrails. The jets blew off part of the wing tip; hit their No. 4 engine propeller, causing severe vibration; and additional hits on the No. 2 and No. 3 engines took their toll.

The crew was not bailed out—several of their parachute packs had been hit during the attack. The pilot landed the aircraft in an open field in Poland where they were taken in tow by Russian soldiers. With their travels and Russian red tape, the crew did not get back to England until April 23.

Reported victories of this battle varied widely, on both sides. Three Me 262s were shot down by the bombers, who claimed eight; while the Luftwaffe pilots claimed twelve heavy bombers, when they actually got six. However, a number of the bombers were total write-offs due to damage incurred. The action by the jets were certainly foreboding for the bomber people, who became vitally concerned after the aggressive performance of JG 7 that day.

MARCH 19, 1945

The following day, bombers were dispatched to strike at synthetic oil refineries and jet aircraft assembly plants. Due to bad weather, only 2nd Air Division B-24s were able to bomb their primary targets, which consisted of jet bases. The Liberators bombed the training field at Neuburg, destroying a number of Me 262s on the ground.

However, before the heavies arrived, two groups of Eighth Air Force fighters went out on sweeps, where they encountered substantial enemy fighter opposition, including a few Me 262s, but primarily conventional fighters.

The 78th Fighter Group ran into a number of Me 109s on their way out and destroyed several of them. As this combat was broken off, two Arado 234 jet bombers appeared on the scene, and they were both destroyed.

The combat report of Lieutenant Allen A. Rosenblum vividly describes a busy morning for a Mustang pilot: "I was flying Surtax Red 3 on a fighter sweep to Berlin, when we encountered three Me 109s in the Osnabruck area. Surtax White Flight tailed one, Surtax Red leader tailed another, and I picked the third.

"I followed him down to 400 feet over an airdrome and fought with him for about ten minutes. I finally broke off in the face of intense, accurate 20 MM and 40 MM flak and because I did not have a wingman. I claim this Me 109 as damaged, as I scored several strikes on his wings.

THE MENACE BECOMES A PROBLEM

"I climbed up and joined Surtax Yellow Flight until we sighted two Ar 234s. We split up, Lieutenant James E. Parker and I taking on one of them. I opened fire at maximum range, but my first shots fell short, so I pulled through him, seeing many strikes around the left jet unit and cockpit. Parker closed in and scored more hits, and the pilot jettisoned his canopy, preparing to bail out. I overran him and chandelled up, completing it in time to see the plane crash into a farmhouse and explode.

"Yellow Flight then re-formed, and we spotted two bogies at nine o'clock low. Yellow leader and Yellow 2 bounced them, not noticing ten others at nine o'clock to the first ones. The bogies were identified as 109s, and all of us closed in for the kill. They broke up into us, and were making head-on passes, when my tail warning unit sounded off. I looked back to see twelve FW 190s bouncing us. I called a break, and we broke into them, making head-on passes. I fired at

Major Niven K. Cranfill following his Me 262 victory on March 19, 1945. At the time, he was commanding officer of the 368th Fighter Squadron, 359th Fighter Group. (Cranfill)

one, and he passed through my line of fire. After the pass, I broke right, watching him slam into the ground. Yellow 3 was out of ammo, so we poured on the coal, climbed up and headed for home."

Rosenblum shared credit for the Ar 234 with Parker. The second Arado was destroyed by Captain Winfield H. Brown and Lieutenant Huie H. Lamb, Jr. Brown made the initial pass on the jet and hit its right jet unit, which ignited and began to emit black smoke. Lamb then came in and set the left jet unit on fire. The pilot jettisoned the canopy but did not get out.

Major Niven K. Cranfill was leading the 368th Fighter Squadron, of the 359th Fighter Group, escorting the bombers when he saw three Me 262s pass over his formation. The Mustang couldn't catch them before they made a pass at a B-17 formation, but after their pass, the jets made a 180-degree turn that put the P-51s in a position to attack. Cranfill pulled in on the tail of one and sprayed its wings with bullets before it sped away.

As he pursued this jet northward, it passed another Me 262 that was heading in the same direction. Apparently, this pilot was throttled back and unaware of the Mustang in pursuit. Cranfill opened fire and riddled the bottom of the fuselage. The jet pilot started a diving turn to the left from which he did not recover.

In the same pattern as the day before, JG 7 got as many of its Me 262s airborne as possible. Forty-five of its planes were airborne and Eighth Air Force INTOPS reported: "… attacks being made by thirty-six Me 262s flying in three waves of twelve, each consisting of four flights flying a vee formation. Enemy aircraft attacked from six to seven o'clock, slightly high, and appeared to be flying at relatively low speeds.

"Although the first wave got through to the bombers, who report attacks by four to seven E/A, escorting fighters arrived on the scene in time to disperse the last two waves, which broke into two ship elements in a slight dive. … Only three bombers were lost to the E/A."

THE MENACE BECOMES A PROBLEM

One of the rescuing Mustangs was piloted by Captain Robert S. Fifield of the 363rd Fighter Squadron, 357th Fighter Group. Fifield reported: "I was leading the second element of Cement Blue Flight, when twenty-plus Me 262s attacked our box from six o'clock, slightly high. I dropped my tanks and tried to beat them to the bombers, but I arrived just as they hit. I shot at about four different ones and finally singled one out. They were all diving away and to the left. They were getting away from me, so I tried lobbing some long-range shots in and finally saw some trailing black smoke.

"The jet slowed down, and I started closing on him. They seemed to fly in elements of two. After I scored more hits, his wingman pulled up close to him, but took off again when I fired in more hits. I closed up to about 400 yards and got many hits. The jet trailed some white smoke, and then went straight in. I never exceeded 400 MPH, and they seemed to be going only 50 MPH faster then us."

Major Robert W. Foy, of the 357th Fighter Group was leading the 364th Fighter Squadron home following escort duties when he sighted three Me 262s in a shallow dive chasing a flight of four P-51s. The Luftwaffe pilots apparently didn't see the Mustangs until they began to close on them. Then they throttled forward and began to pull away. Foy had everything to the firewall, and although he was out of range, he pulled his K-14 sight pip just a bit high and let go two short bursts at the lagging Me 262 in the formation. Surprisingly, the left jet engine on the aircraft began sending back a trail of black smoke. The jet half-rolled to the left and split-essed. The 262 continued in its dive from 6,000 feet and plunged into the ground. The others went into sharper dives and were lost in the haze.

Due to bad weather, Captain Charles H. Spencer and his flight from the 354th Fighter Squadron, of the 355th Fighter Group, had become separated from the balance of their group. Spencer took his flight east of the target and began to sweep back toward the jet bases. On arrival over Giebelstadt airdrome, at 13,000 feet, the Mustang pilots saw an Me 262 come in and land. They orbited several times, then spied a second Me 262 letting down. Spencer took his flight down after it.

Spencer was closing nicely and maneuvered himself in on the tail of the Me 262. The Luftwaffe pilot must have seen him or gotten word that he had an attacker at six o'clock, for he gave his plane full-throttle and began to leave the Mustang behind. Spencer opened fire but saw no strikes.

The 262 pilot led Spencer across Giebelstadt, then tried to pull him across the airdrome at Kitzingen, but the flak was so hot and heavy that the P-51 pilot was forced to break off his pursuit. The German pilot went into a final approach in an attempt to land at Kitzingen. Apparently, though, he forget to lower his gear. About halfway down the runway, the jet hit nose-first and left-wing low. It caught fire immediately after hitting and slid down the runway in flames. As Spencer left the area, a column of smoke rose steadily from the area of the crash.

MARCH 20, 1945

On March 20, Hamburg was the primary target. Once more, fighters went out to sweep the area ahead of the bombers, and once more, the Me 262s from JG 7 flew out to greet them. The 339th Fighter Group met the German jets at 1530 hours in the Hamburg area. Lieutenant Kenneth V. Berguson went after a jet that flew in the opposite direction and managed to close to 800 yards. As the air-craft circled, Berguson fired, scoring a few hits before the 262 disap-peared into the clouds.

Then Berguson and the rest of his flight, led by Lieutenant Jerome J. Ballard, chased another Me 262, which led them over its base at Kaltenkirchen and into heavy fire from 40 MM and 20 MM flak. Bal-lard's Mustang was hit, and he was force to bail out. His parachute did not open fully, but he came down in some trees that broke his fall and was immediately taken prisoner.

As the 303rd Bomb Group came off their target at Hamburg, they were attacked by a force of fifteen to twenty Me 262s. The enemy sometimes pressed their attacks to fifty feet before zooming right through the formation. Most of the jets came in on tail level, although a few came in from the front or side. The fighter escort prevented the attacks from becoming prolonged, but three 303rd Group aircraft sustained major battle damage, seventeen suffered minor damage, and two were downed by the jets.

The B-17 flown by Lieutenant F.R. Taub was flying on the right wing of the high flight leader, in the high 360th Bomb Squadron formation. Three Me 262s shot off the B-17's vertical stabilizer on the first pass. On the second pass, they hit its No. 3 engine and set the right wing on fire. During the attack, some of the crew stated that Sergeant J.L. Hollowell, the ball turret gunner, shot down one of the jets. Both pilots struggled with the controls, so the balance of the crew could bail out. All of the men who escaped the plane became prisoners of war. The two pilots and the waist gunner were killed when the aircraft exploded.

The Fortress flown by Lieutenant T.L. Moore was hit during the jet attack in its No. 2 engine. Chunks of the nacelle tumbled away, and the skin on the left horizontal stabilizer was ripped off. The plane went down in a dive, but when last seen seemed to be under control. For some reason, the two pilots and the engineer gunner were the only survivors.

At 1620 hours, the 505th Fighter Squadron, of the 339th Fighter Group, was flying at 3,000 feet southeast of Hamburg. Captain Harry R. Corey sighted an Me 262 crossing their path. The P-51s went after the jet but scored no hits. Lieutenant Robert E. Irion, who was leading the second element, began to gain when the jet turned to the right. A burst from 700 yards produced some hits. Closing to 600 yards, Irion really began to pepper the jet and knocked off a number of pieces. The 262 went into a shallow dive and began to smoke. The pilot jettisoned his canopy and rolled over to the left. He bailed out, but his parachute did not open. Records indicate that Irion's victim was Unteroffizier Hans Mehn of 1 Staffel, JG 7.

A bit later, the squadron leader for the 504th Fighter Squadron, took his charges down to strafe jet aircraft on the field at Kaltenkirchen. After their strafing runs, the Mustangs formed up, then sighted an Me 262 coming in from six o'clock. Five of the P-51 pilots turned to meet the aircraft head-on. Lieutenant Vernon Barto successfully drove a burst into the left engine nacelle and started a fire. Another burst set the right engine aflame, then an explosion pierced the air. The pilot pulled up, rolled over and bailed out.

MARCH 21, 1945

The majority of the Eighth Air Force bombers were sent to bomb Luftwaffe jet fighter bases on March 21. The Me 262s of JG 7 were scrambled, and numerous combats occurred throughout the morning. In the most important interception, a number of Me 262s attacked B-17s in the vicinity of Plauen, where they had dropped bombs on the motor works.

The jets pressed their attacks to near-collision, hitting the 490th Bomb Group hardest. Lieutenant Lyman D. Shafenberg stated that his tail gunner shot down one of the jets, which was coming in from six o'clock. When hit, the 262 half-rolled over the tail of Shafenberg's Fortress and crashed into the waist section of a B-17 in the element above. The 490th lost three of its Fortresses to the attack, and several others were damaged.

Lieutenant Harry M. Chapman, of the 361st Fighter Group, shot down an Me 262 on March 21, 1945, in the Dresden area, when large numbers of jets intercepted bombers. (USAAF)

THE MENACE BECOMES A PROBLEM

The 100th Bomb Group also felt the wrath of the jets, losing one aircraft to them. The B-17 flown by Lieutenant Bernard Painter went down, and Painter was the only survivor of the crew. Lieutenant Jim Lantz of the 100th recalled: "… About ten minutes after the target, the jets hit us. They came in about five o'clock with their guns blazing, and I could see a fiery stream eating its way up the tail of a ship below and beside me in another squadron. A P-51 was right on the jet's tail with its guns blazing away. I didn't see what happened to the jet but some of the boys said they saw it explode."

Captain Edwin H. Miller of the 83rd Fighter Squadron, 78th Fighter Group, was escorting the bombers when one of the jets was seen firing on the bomber formation. By the time the Mustangs reached the bombers, the jet was coming around for a second pass and firing on the formation. Miller and his wingman went in pursuit at 19,000 feet. The 262 pounced on a cripple that he had previously hit, and Miller fired from 2,000 yards in an attempt to drive him away. He scored a few hits, and the Luftwaffe pilot broke away and down in a dive to the left.

A flight of Mustangs from the 354th Fighter Group caught a flight of Me 262s in the Kassel area on March 2, 1945, and Lieutenant Theodore W. Sedvert was credited with downing one. Sedvert shot up another Me 262 on March 21, and even emptied his .45-caliber pistol into it while flying alongside, before it bellied in. Still, he was not given an official confirmed victory. (USAAF)

GERMAN JETS VS. THE U.S. ARMY AIR FORCE

Miller followed him and started to close, when he realized the jet was headed for the clouds. However, the cloud cover was thin, and when Miller broke through, he spotted his target in a left-hand turn. Miller cut him off and latched onto his tail, where he opened fire from 500 yards. He closed to 100 yards, covering the jet with hits as chunks of the jet flew off. Miller closed further, hitting it with one last, lethal, burst. The jet plummeted straight into the ground.

The yellow-nosed Mustangs of the 361st Fighter Group mixed it up with the Me 262s, too. Lieutenant Harry M. Chapman and his flight saw the jets attacking the bombers, then the aggressive jets came at the Mustangs. As the No. 4 jet pilot turned into Chapman for a head-on pass, the P-51 pilot put the pip of his K-14 sight on his target at 800 yards and opened fire.

His bullets tracked true and began to smash the nose and leading edge left wing, which burst into flames. When the 262 passed Chapman, it was smoking and spiralling down. One of the other flights saw the plane crash and explode.

Lieutenant Richard D. Anderson of the 361st Group also tangled with one of the Me 262s in the same area and managed to shoot it down.

Lieutenant John A. Kirk of the 78th Fighter Group went after one of the jets that was attacking the bombers, using his 5,000-foot advantage to dive down and cut the 262 pilot off when he went into a turn. Kirk opened fire from long-range, but his short bursts paid off. Brown smoke belched from one of the jet engines. The Luftwaffe pilot started into a steep turn to the right and bailed out.

Lieutenant Niles C. Greer and his flight of Mustangs from the 504th Fighter Squadron, of the 339th Fighter Group, had already given up on one Me 262 chase and were on their way home. Suddenly, they saw another Me 262 down below with a P-51, which was far out of range, chasing him. Greer had apparently not been seen— the jet went into a climbing turn to the left that enabled Greer to close easily on the jet. Firing with thirty-degrees deflection, Greer hit the jet in its right engine and wing. The German pilot then went into a fairly tight climbing turn, while Green "continued to give him hell." Bits of the jet tumbled away, and its right engine caught on fire. Greer then let in his No. 3 man, Lieutenant Billy E. Langohr, who scored further hits on the 262, which rolled over and dove straight into the earth.

Shortly after noon, Mustangs from the 82nd Fighter Squadron, of the 78th Fighter Group, arrived over the airdrome at Giebelstadt, where they had a field day. Three Me 262s were caught taking off, and the P-51 pilots went down after them. Lieutenant Robert H. Anderson closed on the last one to take off as it made a large circle to the left. By the time Anderson got in firing range, the jet pilot had led him over the airdrome where heavy flak pierced the air.

The P-51 took some hits but hung on. Unfortunately for the jet pilot, he turned again to lead the Mustang back over the airdrome. When he did, Anderson cut him off and scored with a good long burst into the cockpit. Both aircraft were at only about fifty feet when the Me 262 slammed into the ground and exploded.

Captain Winfield H. Brown and Lieutenant Allen A. Rosenblum went after one of the other Me 262s that had just cleared the ground. They teamed up to shoot it down, although both of them came under heavy light flak from the airdrome.

Lieutenant Walter E. Bourque, of the 78th Fighter Group, got after three Me 262s in the Giebelstadt area and kept after one, even though its formation mates tried to drive him off. Bourque finally caught his victim in a turn and opened fire. Unfortunately, planes from the 339th Group cut him out, but they missed, so Bourque went back after it. He maneuvered himself into a stern attack and clobbered the jet with .50-caliber fire. The plane caught fire, and the left engine exploded. The 262 went down, out of control, pouring smoke from the fuselage and wing.

One of the strangest encounters between an American Mustang and an Me 262 occurred when Captain Theodore W. Sedvert of the

354th Fighter Group, Ninth Air Force, caught a jet from KG (J) 51 down at 500 feet over Osthofen. Sedvert dove on the jet's tail and peppered its tail and fuselage. The German pilot turned and fled at low speed to the east, past the Rhine River. Sedvert discovered that he was now out of ammunition, thanks to a previous dogfight in which he had downed a Focke Wulf 190.

Sedvert caught the Me 262, drew alongside and flew formation with the Luftwaffe pilot, who thumbed his nose at him. This gesture proved to be the last straw for Sedvert, who opened his canopy and emptied his .45-caliber pistol at the aircraft, without result. The Mustang pilot continued to follow the jet until it apparently ran out of fuel and bellied in near the town of Wiesthal.

To raise Sedvert's ire further, the Victories Credits Board refused to confirm his claim for the Me 262: He had not damaged it enough to shoot it down; he had only followed it until it ran out of fuel.

What a busy day for both the jets and the Mustangs. Both had claimed more than they had actually destroyed, but the extensive damage that the jets' 30 MM cannon were inflicting on the bombers was beginning to tell. Even though the Fortresses were managing to fly back to England or often to bases on the Continent, the jet menace was increasing day by day.

Captain William J. Dillard of the Fifteenth Air Force's 31st Fighter Group scored over an Me 262 on March 22, 1945. (USAAF)

THE MENACE BECOMES A PROBLEM

March 22 marked the first day that the Fifteenth Air Force heavy bombers encountered the wrath of the Me 262s. On that morning, 136 B-17s from the 5th Wing rose to attack the oil refinery complex at Ruland, Germany, sixty miles south of Berlin. An estimated twenty-five Me 262s from 3/JG 7 joined conventional-type fighters to combat the raiders. From 1235 to 1310 hours, the jets attacked the bombers.

Hardest hit was the 483rd Bomb Group, which lost six of its Fortresses to the Me 262s, four of them from the 817th Bomb Squadron. A number of the B-17s from that group were also damaged, and several planes returned with wounded aboard.

Lieutenant James H. Kakides, the navigator on the aircraft flown by Lieutenant Con Robinson reported: "We had just hit the target and were in a steep turn to get away from the heavy flak when a huge chunk came right up through my compartment. It missed me by about three inches. The shell burst so close that smoke and powder fumes came into the nose of the plane. … I noticed we were behind the rest of the formation. The next minute, the gunners were calling out fighters on the intercom."

Pilot Robinson related: "The jets came in at us from the rear, six abreast. They made two passes. On the first pass, they scored a few hits but did not do any serious damage. At the same time, Me 109s came in on us from eleven o'clock.

"The 109s did not hurt us, but the jets got on our tail again, and this time they hit us hard. The plane shuddered as the bullets tore into her. A large shell, 30 MM, exploded in the radio room and wounded the radioman severely. The plane got tail heavy and the nose came up, and I forced the controls forward to keep her level. I could smell gas, and I figured our tanks had been punctured and were leaking. The tail kept dropping. The controls got sluggish, and I knew from the way the plane acted that we were hit bad."

Robinson sent Kakides back to the rear to report on the damage there. The 30 MM fire had ripped most of the metal off the horizontal stabilizer, which caused the tail-heaviness. The radioman was suffering from numerous wounds, while the tail gunner, right waist gunner and ball gunner were also wounded. Much of the tail section had been damaged, and the rudder control cables were severed. Two fuel tanks had been hit and were streaming gasoline, making a very volatile situation.

After receiving the status of the aircraft, Robinson told the crew to bail out if they so desired. He was going to try to make it to Russian-held territory before he put the Fortress down in view of the radioman's wounds. The B-17 took another telling flak hit, so Robinson asked Kakides to tell the men to prepare for a crash landing. When the navigator returned to the rear of the plane, he found that all the men, including the radioman, had bailed out.

Robinson managed to make a good crash landing, but little did he know that he had landed right in the front lines. The four crewmembers spent four days in "no man's land" before they could make it to the Russian lines; one of the four did not survive. When reunited with the men who had bailed, they learned that although he had been taken in by the Russians and treated medically, the radioman had succumbed to his wounds. The eight surviving crewmembers returned to their unit in Italy thirty-three days after their harrowing mission.

As to the fate of the sixty-one men who fell to the guns of the jets that day: Seventeen were killed in action, twenty-seven were made prisoners of war, and seventeen made their way back to the group.

Three Me 262s also attacked a formation of B-17s from the 97th Bomb Group. Only one pass was made from the rear, but the jet's 30 MM guns destroyed the controls and autopilot of the Fortress flown by Lieutenant Charles G. Getzloff. Four crewmembers were killed in the attack, the copilot and three of the gunners. The aircraft went into a spin and the balance of the crew bailed out.

THE MENACE BECOMES A PROBLEM

The jets were intercepted by Mustangs from the escorting 31st Fighter Group, who destroyed one of the jets and damaged several others. Captain William Dillard and his wingman were flying at 26,000 feet when they sighted two Me 262s a thousand feet below.

Dillard reported: "I dove to attack and fired from out of range in an effort to make them break off from the bombers. After making their attack, one enemy aircraft broke left, the other right. I chased the one that broke right into a gentle dive, continuing to fire at the extreme range of 1,000 to 1,200 yards.

"At about 10,000 feet, I saw small hunks fly from the left side of the jet, and I began to close rapidly. When we reached 7,000 to 8,000 feet, I was firing from 400 to 500 yards away, and the enemy aircraft took some slight evasive action, composed mostly of turns and climbs. I closed to 300 yards, firing away, and at 6,000 feet, the jet's left power unit caught fire. The pilot jettisoned the canopy, rolled the plane on its side and bailed out."

The same day, the Eighth Air Force sent its bombers after military barracks, encampments and airfields in central Germany. At 1230 hours, Lieutenant John W. Cunnick, of the 38th Fighter Squadron, 55th Fighter Group, caught an Me 262 taking off from the airfield at Lechfeld. However, the camouflage paint scheme on the jet paid off in this instance—the Mustangs lost it against the surface background.

A few minutes later, Cunnick spotted another 262 trying to get in for a landing. The P-51 pilot dropped his tanks and went down after the jet. Cunnick began to fire while still out of range, but he continued firing until he had closed to 300 yards. The 262 pilot had tightened his turns over the field, and Cunnick was unable to hit the jet until it went into a quarter snap roll to the inside, which permitted him to fire right at the cockpit. As a result of this telling blast, the pilot, possibly Oberfeldwebel Helmut Recker of III/EJG 2, flew right into the ground.

Lieutenant Milton B. Stutzman, of the 78th Fighter Group, was escorting the bombers near Ulm when he spotted an Me 262 that was attacking his charges. The jet pilot had sighted the Mustangs at about the same time and broke off his attack to flee south. When the jet was almost out of sight from the P-51s, the pilot sent his aircraft into a gentle ninety-degree turn to the right, no doubt thinking that he was safe and sound. This enabled the Mustang pilot to cut him off and close on him.

At that moment, the jet pilot did a 180 and came right back into the face of the P-51s. With only Stutzman hanging on, the 262 pilot headed north for an airdrome near Lake Constance and led him across the middle of it. Stutzman fired at the jet all the way across the field, and it finally began to smoke badly. The pilot got rid of his canopy and bailed out, but Stutzman never saw his chute open.

As the 262 began its dive to earth, Lieutenant Eugene L. Peel also bored in on the aircraft, firing away. He was awarded half the victory.

Captain Harold T. Barnaby of the 78th Fighter Group was fortunate enough to catch a flight of four Me 262s preparing to take off from the airdrome at Giebelstadt. Barnaby dove from 10,000 feet down to 1,000 feet, where he caught a jet and opened fire. His first burst hit the left engine, which exploded. The pilot used his speed to climb up to about 2,000 feet, where he went over the side. The victim was probably Unteroffizier Adabert Egri of 1/KG (J) 54, who was wounded in the attack, but landed safely in his parachute.

The jets pilots claimed twelve bombers downed for the day, but only seven B-17s of the Fifteenth Air Force actually fell to their guns, although many of the B-17s returned to Italy with serious damage. Six jets fell victim to the fighters and bombers, while five were claimed by fighter pilots.

MARCH 23, 1945

The B-17s of the Fifteenth Air Force returned to Ruhland on March 23, bombing the target with excellent results. Only three B-17s were lost on the mission, and all of these were reportedly lost to flak. Me 262s were seen in the area, but no encounters were reported officially.

MARCH 24, 1945

March 24 marked the Allies' Operation Varsity, the last massive airborne operation in Europe. Paratroops and glider infantry were landed across the Rhine River, as massive numbers of fighter and bombers from the Eighth Air Force covered the area in its support.

To draw some of the Luftwaffe opposition away from the area, the Fifteenth Air Force dispatched 150 B-17s to bomb the Daimler-Benz Tank Works in Berlin. This mission was at the extreme end of range for the Fortresses, so its pilots had been briefed to make only one bomb run— they would not have sufficient fuel to fly home if they made a second run.

The 463rd Bomb Group led the 5th Wing on the operation, but unfortunately, the group ran into an intense flak barrage west of Brux that was not on the flak map. Four of their Fortresses went down, and two oth-

When the Fifteenth Air Force flew its first mission to Berlin on March 24, 1945, Colonel William Daniel, commanding officer of the 31st Fighter Group, led his Mustangs to one of the unit's six victories over Me 262s for the day. (USAF)

ers were so badly damaged that those aircraft had to abort the mission. As the rest of the bombers journeyed on toward the target, they were attacked by fifteen Me 262s, which downed one of the B-17s and damaged a number of others.

Also attacked by jets was the 483rd Bomb Group, which lost one Fortress during the initial onslaught by the jets. One of the bombers that was caught up in the fight was a B-17 called *Big Yank*, flown by Lieutenant William Strapko. Four of the Me 262s came in on the craft, which was flying "tail-end Charlie," and began to exchange fire with the gunners on the crew.

Staff Sergeant Lincoln Broyhill, the tail gunner, reported that two of the jets closed on him firing and did not break until they were within 200 yards. Broyhill said: "I had seen my tracers going into his fuselage, and I'm sure he was badly hit. The minute the first fighter turned away, the second came boring in. Again, I had to keep my guns going, and again, at about 200 yards it turned away, then it went spiraling down. My guns then jammed because they had been firing too long."

The copilot, Lieutenant Clair Harper, was watching and hoping that they would survive the enemy fire, when he glanced to his left and saw an Me 262 headed straight for *Big Yank*. The top turret gunner, Staff Sergeant Howard Wehner, was firing at one jet, then turned to open up on the 262 that seemed headed for a collision with the Fortress. Harper yelled to his pilot, "Bill, he's going to ram us!" Wehner continued to fire his .50 calibers, and when only thirty yards away, the jet suddenly pulled up and exploded.

The crew of *Big Yank* was credited with downing three Me 262s in the scrap, two of them were awarded to Wehner.

While the jets from JG 7 and 3/EJG 2 had the bombers under attack, they were intercepted by Mustangs from the 332nd and then the 31st Fighter Group. Lieutenant Roscoe C. Brown of the 100th Fighter Squadron reported: "We were flying at 27,000 feet, when at 1215 hours, we noticed three Me 262s coming at the bombers from eleven o'clock. The jets were attacking individually rather than in formation. I called for the flight to drop tanks, and we peeled off, right on the three Me 262s. I fired at one from 2,400 feet, spotting him right in the extreme range of my K-14 gunsight. He went into a dive, and I went with him to 23,000 feet, where I broke off pursuit due to the exceptional diving speed of the jet.

"I climbed back to 27,000 feet, and I sighted a formation of four Me 262s under the bombers at about 24,000 feet. They were below me going north. I was going south. I peeled down on them toward their rear, but almost immediately I saw a lone 262 at 24,000 feet, climbing at ninety degrees to me and 2,500 feet from me. I pulled up at him in a fifteen-degree climb and fired three long bursts from 2,000 feet, at eight o'clock to him. Almost immediately, the pilot bailed out—from 24,500 feet. I saw flames burst from the jet orifices of the enemy aircraft."

Lieutenant Charles V. Brantley and his flight leader from the 100th Squadron noticed two Me 262s flying down below them and dove on them. Brantley fired several bursts from directly astern before the two jets broke in slow turns in opposite directions. The Mustang pilot continued to follow his jet and scored hits on the fuselage. The 262 then went into a high-speed dive, but Brantley's flight leader and several other pilots saw it continue down in flames.

Lieutenant Earl R. Lane, also from the 100th Fighter Squadron, caught an Me 262 as it came across the bomber formation. He came in and fired using thirty-degrees deflection from 2,000 feet. Following three short bursts, a large chunk flew off and the craft began to smoke as it plunged down. Lane circled the area and saw it crash as a smudge of black smoke rose from below.

Two further 262s were claimed probably destroyed and two more damaged by the pilots from the 332nd Group. However, in the fight they lost three pilots: Lieutenants Robert C. Robinson and Ronald W. Reeves, who were killed, and Captain Armour G. McDaniel, who became a prisoner of war. Additionally, Lieutenant Leon W. Spears' Mustang was so severely damaged that he was forced to land in Russian-occupied territory. Lieutenant Hannibal Cox, despite missing about one foot off the end of one wing, managed to get on the deck and make it home.

About the time the 332nd Group broke off its fight with the jets, the 31st Fighter Group arrived. Colonel William A. Daniel, the Commanding Officer of the unit, was leading and he stated: "At 1225 hours, from 28,000 feet just south of the target, I observed two Me 262s headed toward the bombers from eleven o'clock. The bombers were headed north, the enemy fighters were headed east and I was headed west, putting me 180 degrees from the enemy aircraft and ninety degrees from the bombers.

"As I saw the two enemy aircraft turn into the bombers from astern, I turned in and started to close and fire, however, I observed four more enemy aircraft turning in. I waited for the No. 6 enemy aircraft to turn, then closed in on him from about four-thirty o'clock to 500 yards and fired. No strikes were observed, although the enemy aircraft snap-rolled and went into a spin. I observed a parachute and four blobs of smoke."

Lieutenant Forrest M. Keene of the 308th Fighter Squadron was element leader to Lieutenant Raymond D. Leonard. They were flying at 28,000 feet, when they spotted two Me 262s headed for the bombers. The two Mustangs dove down to 25,000 feet and pulled out with a jet on Keene's six o'clock. Leonard told him he would take care of it, leaving Keene free to pursue the other Me 262, which was making a pass at the bombers. Keene closed on the tail of the jet, and opened fire at 500 yards. The 262 went down in a diving turn to the left, streaming smoke.

True to his word, Leonard took care of the 262 on his leader's tail. He pulled in under and to the rear of the jet and opened fire at 200 yards. Hits were scored on the left engine and pieces flew off. The pilot turned his aircraft into a gentle climb and bailed out.

Captain Kenneth T. Smith, also of the 308th Fighter Squadron, caught three Me 262s going after the bombers from underneath. He dove down and pulled up in a position slightly above one of the jets, opening fire from 300 yards. The pilot was seen to bail out.

Lieutenant William M. Wilder was the fourth Mustang pilot from the 308th to score. As one of the jets came in at nine o'clock to a Fortress, Wilder went down and came in on its tail. He closed to 150 yards, getting multiple hits on its fuselage, wings and right engine. As the jet began to stream smoke, the pilot went over the side.

It had been a most profitable mission for the 31st Fighter Group. They were awarded five confirmed destroyed, and three Me 262s damaged, with no losses.

Total claims for the day are very conflicting. Pilots from JG 7 claimed at least nine bombers downed, while only two fell to their guns. The gunners on the bombers claimed six Me 262s destroyed, when JG 7 says that only one was hit by the bomber crewmen. Eight confirmed victories were credited to the Mustang pilots, while JG 7 says they only lost two, with a third pilot wounded who made it home safely.

Lieutenant Raymond M. Littge, of the 352nd Fighter Group, downed an Me 262 over Rechlin airdrome on March 25, 1945. (USAAF)

The fact that the jets were becoming a bigger problem was pointed out by the Commanding General of the Eighth Air Force, General Jimmie Doolittle. During an Air Commander's Conference held in late March, Doolittle stated: "The threat that we have been anticipating has now materialized. Jets are now attacking in formations as large as thirty-six aircraft and are using more effective tactics. Besides attacking the bombers, they are attacking the fighter escort immediately on penetration in the hopes of making them drop their tanks." Doolittle set up attacks against the jet airfields to be carried out the last week in March.

MARCH 25, 1945

On March 25, all three divisions of Eighth Air Force bombers were sent out to attack oil plants, but bad weather forced the 1st and 3rd Air Divisions to abort their missions. The Liberators of the 2nd Air Division continued on to strike at their targets. Me 262s from both JG 7 and KG (J) 54 intercepted the B-24s.

Taking the brunt of the onslaught was the 448th Bomb Group, which was hit during their run in from the Initial Point. The jets shot down one squadron leader immediately, while downing two other B-24s over the target, which was the underground oil storage depot at Hitzaker. Another B-24 suffered extensive damage and went down shortly thereafter. The other two squadrons of the 448th were struck as they came off the target, and ten B-24s were damaged by the Me 262s' lethal 30 MM guns.

Mustangs from the 479th Fighter Group arrived on the scene to intercept the enemy. Lieutenant Eugene H. Wendt reported: "Just as we got to a point three o'clock high to the bombers, I saw two Me 262s closing on the tail box of bombers from five o'clock, slightly high to them at an altitude of about 21,000 feet. I immediately ordered my section to drop tanks and made a right diving turn to get in position on the jets. Before I could maneuver into position, however, the lead jet attacked the bombers and shot down two of them, then it pulled up in a steep right climbing turn.

"As the Me 262 did this, I was attempting to dump my belly tanks, which wouldn't come off. I dove head-on at the jet, anyway. Closing to about 1,200 yards, and with seventy-degrees deflection, I gave him a short burst. I didn't see any strikes and the enemy aircraft continued his climb. I pulled up very sharply and swung around onto his tail. I fired a couple of good bursts from 1,000 yards with seventy-degrees deflection.

"I gave him a short burst and closed my curve of pursuit and fired a long burst from 500 to 200 yards, thirty- to ten-degrees deflection, observing strikes all over the fuselage, cockpit and wing roots. Then, I fired another burst from dead astern, at fifty feet or less, before I passed him. The Me 262 went into a spin and flames streamed out from around the cockpit. I started to follow, but lost control momentarily of my plane and had my hands full with it."

Wendt's victim was probably Feldwebel Taube, who was shot down and killed right after destroying a Liberator.

Lieutenant Raymond H. Littge of the 352nd Fighter Group went after an Me 262 in the target area, but gave up after a fifteen-minute chase. Littge stayed out of sight for a while, and then pulled up directly over Rechlin airdrome. He was rewarded with the presence of an Me 262 coming in over the field. As the jet pilot dropped his landing gear, Littge made a firing pass but observed no hits. The Mustang pilot then leveled off behind the 262 and opened fire, and several long bursts set the right engine burning.

Thunderbolts of the 56th Fighter Group also encountered the Me 262s that day. Captain George E. Bostwick and some of his flight pursued a number of jets that sped eastwards and attempted to land on the airfield at Parchim. Bostwick came after one of the 262s as it dropped down over the runway. Instead of landing, however, the 262 flew straight down the runway.

As it reached the end of the runway, the jet passed another Me 262 that had just taken off. Bostwick pulled his nose through to fire on this new target, but the pilot made a tight turn to the left. As he did so, his left wing dug into the ground and the aircraft cart-wheeled, breaking apart and strewing wreckage across the field.

Bostwick went back after his original target and got in a telling burst from 800 yards, but the Me 262 continued to speed away from him.

Joining the jet chase with Bostwick was Lieutenant Edwin Crosth-wait, who had sighted a 262 flying over Parchim on their arrival. This jet, though, soon sped away from him, too. Crosthwait continued to orbit and soon saw the 262 returning to the area, apparently the aircraft was low on fuel and the pilot was trying to land. Crosth-wait turned inside the aircraft as the pilot turned onto his final approach, then fired, but he didn't see any hits.

The 262 leveled out on its final approach to the runway, and the Mustang pilot closed to 500 yards on its tail. Strikes immediately registered on the right engine, and the pilot went over the side while the aircraft continued down to crash. His victim was probably Oberfahn-rich Ullrich, who was killed following his bail out because he was too low for his parachute to completely open.

In total, the four claims against Me 262s by the

Lieutenant Colonel John D. Landers led the 78th Fighter Group on a very aggressive offensive against the jets. He shared an Me 262 on the afternoon of March 30, 1945. (Landers)

THE MENACE BECOMES A PROBLEM

fighters can be confirmed, but in reality, seven jets were lost that day, five from JG 7 and two from KG (J) 54.

In all probability, the other three were downed by bomber crews. As for the bombers, only the four B-24s from the 448th Bomb Group fell victims to the jets that day.

MARCH 30, 1945

Following several days of bad weather, the Eighth Air Force bombers set out for targets in Germany. On this day, the Allies struck targets that involved U-boat operations at Hamburg, Bremen and Wilhelmshafen. JG 7 put up serviceable Me 262s to intercept, and several sharp actions resulted.

The 339th Fighter Group was involved early on. As Colonel John B. Henry, Jr., the Group Commanding Officer, led his charges at 29,000 feet, two bogies were spotted down below. As Henry began to lead his Mustangs down to investigate, he sighted an Me 262 on its way up.

Henry continued to dive and fired a long burst at the jet at 22,000 feet. Strikes were seen, and dark smoke belched from both engines as the jet escaped into the clouds.

Captain Jim Starnes was leading the 505th Fighter Squadron's Upper Yellow Flight northeast of Hamburg when they were jumped from above. A break was called, but the pilot who called the message used the wrong flight color and Upper Yellow Flight did not break. Lieutenant Evergard L. Wager, flying Yellow Two, was hit and his Mustang was set on fire. Wager bailed out, but his parachute streamed and never fully opened.

A short time later, nine Me 262s passed head-on through the 504th Fighter Squadron. The P-51s broke immediately, and sped after their attackers, but to no avail. After giving up the chase, Captain Robert F. Sargent joined up with Lieutenant Leonard A. Kunz, and they returned to the target area. As they passed over

Kaltenkirchen airdrome, they saw two Me 262s taking off and dove down on them. Sargent closed on the tail of the rearmost jet and fired, getting good hits. White smoke poured back from one engine, and the cockpit canopy was jettisoned. Lieutenant Erich Schutle of 1/Gruppe JG 7 bailed out, but he was too low for his chute to open. The second jet gained speed rapidly, and left the Mustangs behind.

Meanwhile, Lieutenant Carroll W. Bennett broke into two Me 262s and scored several hits on one of them, before he lost them both in the clouds at 8,000 feet. Bennett dropped below the clouds, but could not find his jet. Climbing, Bennett found another Me 262, and began to chase it. From Bad Oldsloe to Bad Segeberg, then southeast to Lubeck, the jet flew, with Bennett scoring hits all along the way. Near Lubeck, the jet finally began to blaze and dove into the clouds.

Lieutenant Patrick L. Moore of the 55th Fighter Group also engaged the jets in the target area of Hamburg. After futilely chasing a jet with his fellow Mustang pilots, Moore wound up flying by himself. He finally found another flight from the 55th Group and joined up with them as they proceeded to Lubeck airfield. While the one flight flew on the north side of the field, Moore went to the south side. There, he spied an Me 262 coming in to land. Moore dove down in a high-speed pass from astern, scoring many hits. The jet hit the runway, nosed up, skidded to the right and finally turned over on its back.

Lieutenant Colonel John D. Landers was leading his 78th Fighter Group out after an escort duty to Hamburg. While flying at 7,000 feet in the vicinity of Rendsburg, Landers saw an Me 262 flying below, at 1,000 feet. As the Mustang pilot closed on the jet, it banked left and led the P-51s over the airfield at Hahn, where they encountered light flak.

Landers opened fire at 700 yards, hitting one engine, which slowed the 262 down. The Luftwaffe pilot then made the fatal mistake of turning, and Landers hit him again from 400 yards. The 262 went into a steep bank and took the next burst in the cockpit.

Following that burst, Landers overran his target. The jet leveled out and went into a gentle glide. Then, Lander's wingman, Lieutenant Thomas V. Thain, Jr., pulled in astern of the Me 262 and administered a final burst to the jet, which crashed and burned.

Lieutenant Kenneth J. Scott, Jr., of the 361st Fighter Group, was leading a flight on patrol over the Schleswing Peninsula, at 12,000 feet, when he saw a jet at eleven o'clock heading toward his squadron. The Me 262 was in a dive, so Scott started a diving turn to intercept. He succeeded in cutting the 262 off and wound up about 200 yards behind, at sixty degrees to the enemy craft.

Once more, a Luftwaffe jet made the fatal mistake of maneuvering into a turn while being pursued by a Mustang. Scott closed the distance and wound up at ten degrees to the craft, at only 200 yards. A long burst from the Mustang pilot ripped through the jet, whose pilot stood up and bailed out.

Another long chase took place when Lieutenant James C. Hurley went after an Me 262 just north of Magdeburg. The 352nd Fighter Group pilot dropped his tanks and attacked. Although he had an altitude advantage, Hurley could not approach within firing range at any time during a twenty-minute chase.

Apparently, though, the jet finally ran out of fuel and both its engines quit. The 262 pilot went into a turn from about 6,000 feet, but the P-51 pilot was right on top of him. Hurley fired until he was within fifty yards of the 262, when the jet suddenly nosed over and went straight in from 5,000 feet.

The last jet victory of the day came when Lieutenant John B. Guy, of the 364th Fighter Group, and a pilot from the 352nd Fighter Group chased an Me 262 that had just fired on a bomber. As the two Mustangs closed on the enemy aircraft, the 352nd pilot put some telling shots into the jet's left engine, and it went into a left bank. Guy cut inside and let go with a burst that knocked large pieces off the aircraft, which began to trail heavy smoke. The Luftwaffe pilot rolled the jet over on its back and went out.

All total, the Mustang pilots claimed seven Me 262s destroyed, one probably destroyed and five damaged for the day. Three Mustangs were lost, one positively lost to an Me 262. Three bombers on the Hamburg attack were lost. One of the most notable losses for the Luftwaffe was Leutnant Karl Schnorrer, a Knights Cross winner with thirty-five victories in the East and credit for nine four-engined bombers as leader of 2/JG 7. Schnorrer was hit by fire from the bombers after he claimed two of them, and then he was forced to bail out when attacked by a bevy of Mustangs. In doing so, he struck the tail of his aircraft, severely injuring his leg.

MARCH 31, 1945

On March 31, Eighth Air Force bombers attacked oil targets, but most of the jets' attention was turned to daylight raids that were made by the Royal Air Force. JG 7 got into a Lancaster formation and claimed large numbers of downed.

Only a small number of the Me 262s engaged the Eighth Air Force bombers, and they claimed three B-17s downed. However, two of the B-17s lost that day fell to flak. Lieutenant Harrison B. Tordoff was leading a flight from the 352nd Fighter Squadron, of the 353rd Fighter Group, when two Me 262s passed below them.

The Mustangs went screaming down, using speed built up from their altitude advantage to catch the jets. Tordoff began firing from 700 yards and managed to strike the left engine of the aircraft, but it still pulled away from him. The P-51s continued to pursue the jets for some time, hoping they would run short of fuel and have to find a landing ground.

When the jets did reach an airdrome, the Mustangs were still two miles behind. The two jets split up, and two P-51s went after the craft with the good engines while Tordoff went after his original target. As Tordoff began to close on the Me 262, it pulled up in a steep climb and the left engine ignited. The pilot jettisoned the canopy and went over the side.

Pilots from the 78th Fighter Group happened upon a few jets during their escort mission, and finally found one they could chase. After a long and uneventful quest, most of the Mustangs gave up. However, the persistence of Lieutenant Wayne L. Colemon paid off.

He spied an Me 262 slightly below and ahead of him, so he split-essed and closed rapidly on the jet. His first burst hit the right engine and cockpit area. The Me 262 pulled up, causing Coleman to break to the left, then it rolled to the right and slammed straight into the ground.

The 2nd Scouting Force also moved into the scoring column again on the thirty-first, when two of its pilots were attacked by Me 262s in the vicinity of Brunswick. During the scrap, Lieutenant Marvin L. Castleberry was credited with destroying one of the Me 262s.

That morning, a Ninth Air Force Thunderbolt pilot caught one of KG (J) 54's Me 262s as it took off from Giebelstadt. Captain William T. Bales, Jr., of the 371st Fighter Group, surprised the jet just after it had taken off. A sharp burst from the eight .50 calibers of the P-47 was all it took to send the enemy aircraft back to earth.

March had been a busy month for both the Me 262 units and for the escorting aircraft of the Eighth Air Force. The tactics the jet pilots had been using, in which they came in below the bombers, had been quite successful. The escort fighters usually flew above the bomber stream, and often the bombers had already been hit and were going down before the escort knew the attackers were there.

The biggest shortcoming of the Luftwaffe pilots was that they did not to use their superior speed to escape the Mustangs rather than turning back into them, which put the jet pilot at a decided disadvantage. The Me 262 units were also plagued during March by lack of replacement parts, due to concentrated attacks on their airfields. However, their numbers continued to buildup, just in time for the climax that would come in April.

CHAPTER 5

THE MENACE—CLIMAX AND DEMISE

O n April 1, 1945, the Western Allies began to push into Germany and overrun many of the jet bases. The Russian offensives were in full swing, and as they swept in from the east, the Third Reich was locked in a vise that grew smaller and smaller by the day.

KG (J) 51 had been forced to move to bases in Bavaria, Riem, Furth and Memmingen. It was joined at Riem-Munich by General Galland and JV 44. 1/JG 7 left Kaltenkirchen for Briest, Burg and Oranienburg.

APRIL 4, 1945

Weather curtailed aerial operations the first few days in April, and it was the fourth of the month before American forces were able to engage the jet units to any extent. One of the first combats of the day involved an old Twelfth Air Force fighter unit that had joined the 1st Tactical Air Force in France in late 1944 and had been operating from Luneville, France, since January of 1945. At 0900 hours on the April 4, Lieutenant Mortimer J. Thompson, of the 316th Fighter Squadron, came upon an Arado 234 in the Augsburg area and shot it down.

Bomber operations for the Eighth Air Force were directed at the jet airfields. Prior to the arrival of the bombers, the 339th Fighter Group made an early morning sweep over the home of 3/JG 7 at Parchim. The Mustangs were airborne at 0705 hours and were over the airdrome by 0915. Lieutenant Colonel William C. Clark, who led the mission, left most of his charges above the clouds as top cover while he took his flight down to the deck to attack the airdrome.

The jets had already been alerted, so Major Rudolf Sinner, with six more Me 262s, took off and led the formation out. They met with Clark down on the deck head-on. The Mustangs broke immediately to pursue the jets, and Clark let go a burst that got a few strikes on one of the jets. However, all the jets escaped into the clouds.

As Sinner and two other Me 262s rose through a hole in the clouds, they came under attack from Captain Kirke B. Everson and Lieutenant Robert C. Croker. Sinner immediately dove for the clouds with the two P-51s right behind. When they broke out of the clouds, the jet was only 350 yards in front of them at 2,000 feet.

The Mustang pilots fired two bursts that ignited the jet's right engine. Sinner again took to the clouds for cover, but when he came out, the P-51s were still there. Sinner bailed out at 900 feet and floated to ground near the burning wreckage of his aircraft.

Lieutenant Robert C. Havinghurst went after one of the other Me 262s that had come up through the clouds. He began a dive from above the jet and followed the aircraft as it went into a left turn, then a 180-degree turn, back to the airfield. Havinghurst was firing on the 262 while it maneuvered and scored solid strikes on its left engine.

The 262 pilot took his craft down through the clouds, where the Mustang pilot found himself in heavy flak. Havinghurst dropped his tanks so he could take evasive action. The 262 pulled up through a break in the clouds, and the P-51 pilot opened fire again, hitting the cockpit area. Black smoke began to stream from the jet's left engine. At 2,000 feet, the 262 nosed over and went straight down. When last seen, it was still in a vertical dive from 1,000 feet.

Also in on the bounce of the 262s that came up through the hole in the clouds was Captain Nile C. Greer from the 504th Fighter Squadron. Greer stated: "I had about 4,000 feet altitude on them and therefore closed in easily. ... I got the one on the left in my pipper and fired a short burst. The enemy aircraft immediately flipped over into a reversed turn to the left, and I really nailed him, observing plenty of hits behind the cockpit and on both units [engines]. He ducked through a tall cumo [cloud]. I pulled up over it, and there he was.

"With a long burst, I observed hits all over his units and wing roots. Black smoke started to pour from both units, by this time heavily, and tracer flak was really popping around me. The pilot jettisoned his canopy but did not jump. I fired a short burst that must have fired his pants—he lost no time in bailing out. I did not observe his chute, but my two wingmen did."

A short time later, Captain Harry R. Corey, of the 339th's 505th Fighter Squadron, was sweeping the Gummerower Lake area at 2,000 feet when he sighted an Me 262 at ten o'clock. Corey turned into the craft, pulled up and fired without obvious results. Corey pulled up again and went after the jet, but it raced into the clouds. A chase began during which the 262 pilot reversed direction several times with the Mustang staying right on his rear.

A full five-second burst sent fuel streaming back from the left engine and hunks flew off the right wing. Suddenly, the 262 snap-rolled twice and fell off into a flat spin from 1,500 feet. The pilot jettisoned his canopy but never bailed out.

Lieutenant Colonel George F. Ceuleers led the A Group, of the 364th Fighter Group, on an escort mission for B-17s that dropped Disney bombs on a U-boat pen at Hamburg. Ceuleers and his Mustangs were on the way home from the mission, when he saw inbound B-24s under attack from enemy aircraft.

His box of B-17s was protected by the B Group, of the 364th, as well as the A Group, so Ceuleers took his Mustangs over to break up the attack on the Liberators. The attackers proved to be eight Me 262s flying in pairs and coming in from the south.

Ceuleers had an altitude advantage on the Me 262 that he went after, and he set his power to 3,000 RPM, pulling sixty inches of manifold pressure. He and his flight formed up at six o'clock to the Me 262 and away they went. Ceuleers stated that the wash from the jet engines caused him a lot of trouble, but he hung in and chased the Me 262 for twenty minutes. He finally closed to a range of 500 yards and opened fire.

THE MENACE—CLIMAX AND DEMISE

When he was only 100 yards behind the jet, the only damage that the Mustang pilot had noted was some chunks that flew off. Finally, the jet pilot nosed up and jettisoned his canopy, which flung back and hit the right wing of the Mustang. Then the pilot bailed out over Ceuleers' left wing. The aircraft went in from about 500 feet.

The B Group of the 4th Fighter Group was escorting the bombers, when the Liberators were hit by the Me 262s. Lieutenant Raymond A. Dyer was leading Cobweb Green Flight, when he saw a 262 maneuvering for an attack on the bombers from five o'clock and went down after it.

Opening fire from 800 yards and closing to 600 yards, he ripped the jet with a three-second burst into the cockpit area.

Lieutenant Colonel George Ceuleers, of the 364th Fighter Group, chased an Me 262 more than 180 miles before he finally brought it down near Munich on April 4, 1945. (USAAF)

Dyer then came under fire from the bombers and had to break off, but a short while later, he noticed that the jet was smoking. The 262 flew straight and level for a few seconds, went into a dive and started to spin. The aircraft continued to earth and blew up on contact.

Lieutenant Harold H. Frederick of the 4th Group also went after one of the Me 262s that were after the B-24s. He spiraled down on the tail of the jet and opened fire from 300 yards, closing to 75 yards. Multiple hits were made, but the left engine took the most damage and burst into flames. Frederick overshot, pulled up to the right and flipped back to the left to make another pass, but by this time Lieutenant Michael J. Kennedy was firing on it. Kennedy's hits clobbered the right engine, and the jet went down blazing.

Even though the Mustangs had done a good job of downing the Me 262s, the bombers had still taken losses. The 93rd Group lost one Liberator, and the 448th lost three. The jets came in on the bombers while they flew between the Initial Point and the target. Captain John Ray's Liberator blew up—no survivors. Lieutenant Bob Mains, of the 714th Squadron, and his crew bailed out, and Lieutenant Jim Shafer, also from the 714th Squadron, and his crew were last seen going down with two engines on fire. A fourth B-24 from the 448th limped home badly damaged.

Lieutenant Elmer H. Ruffle of the 357th Fighter Squadron, 355th Fighter Group, was leading a flight in the vicinity of Magdeburg later that morning when he saw a jet aircraft approaching his area. Ruffle immediately went down to cut it off and opened fire on the craft he had identified as an Arado 234.

He hit it from 800 yards, and as he closed, the aircraft began to trail smoke. The Luftwaffe pilot continued turning, enabling the Mustang pilot to close more each time. Finally, the 234 went into a steep bank, and Ruffle struck it full in the cockpit. The jet turned over on its back and plummeted down.

The 324th Fighter Group claimed its second jet of the day when Lieutenant John W. Haun mixed it up with four Me 262s, downing one of them. Later in the day, eight Thunderbolts from the 324th caught another Me 262 taking off from the field at Memmingen. As one flight went down, Lieutenant Ryland T. Dewey caught another Me 262 over the field and knocked some pieces off before it escaped into the clouds.

Lieutenant Andrew Kandis led the flight that had gone down after the jet that was taking off. They closed rapidly on the 262, which was desperately trying to gain some speed. A long burst struck all over the plane, and its flaps dropped. As Kandis pulled in, still firing, chunks flew off the jet and its left wing root disintegrated in flames. The aircraft was consumed by fire and it crashed on the airfield.

In a very active day, JG 7 had put nearly fifty 262s in the air; they lost eight of them, and five returned with battle damage. Eighth Air Force Mustang pilots claimed six Me 262s, with another twenty claimed as damaged and one probably destroyed. Four B-24 Liberators had fallen to the jets. Four Eighth Air Force Mustangs were lost, but none of them fell to jets. The 324th Fighter Group of the 1st Tactical Air Force entered their first jet claims, with two Arado 234s and one Me 262 destroyed, and another Me 262 damaged.

APRIL 5, 1945

On April 5, Bombers from the Eighth Air Force went back after airfields as well as marshalling yards. The jets were not up in great numbers, but those that were fought quite successfully. B-17s of the 1st Air Division were intercepted by Me 262s from JV 44, and the division lost one Fortress from the 379th Bomb Group, while several other were severely damaged.

One tactic used by JV 44 had been rehearsed earlier by some of the pilots against a captured Fortress. They found that in an overhead attack, the computing Sperry sight in the upper turret could not track fast enough to keep them framed on a zoom out. When making what was often nearly a surprise pass from above and the rear, they were able to fire effectively, then zoom upwards protected from the guns of the upper turret.

B-24s from the 2nd Air Division were attacked over central Germany. Fast and furious overhead attacks from six o'clock knocked down at least four and possibly five of them.

The Mustangs got in few intercepts during the day due to clouds and scattered small jet formations. The one confirmed jet victory recorded for April 5 was credited to Captain John C. Fahringer, a Thunderbolt pilot from the 56th Fighter Group's 63rd Fighter Squadron. An Me 262 pilot made a pass at the bombers from three o'clock to nine o'clock and started a turn to the right, apparently unaware that a flight of Thunderbolts sat 3,000 feet above him.

The flight of P-47s dropped their tanks and started down with Lieutenant Phillip Kuhn on the inside. Kuhn was able to fire, but he overshot the aircraft. Fahringer rolled out on the tail of the 262 and opened fire. He saw no results of his initial bursts, but the jet pilot went into the fatal turn, enabling the P-47 pilot to cut the distance.

The Luftwaffe pilot tried desperately to get into a cloud, but he was thwarted by insufficient cover. When he came out, the Thunderbolt was only 500 yards behind. Additional fire knocked hunks off the enemy aircraft, and as smoke began to stream, Fahringer saw something pass out to the right—the pilot had bailed out.

April 7, Day of the Rammjager

No air-to-air action occurred on April 6, but the following day made up for the lack—a day that would become known as the Day of the Rammjager. A number of Luftwaffe pilots had volunteered to become ramming pilots, whose assignment was to bash into American bombers in order to down them.

This desperate tactic included an attempt to cut into the Allied bomber's aft portion, just behind the wing, with the German fighter pilot using his aircraft's wing like a cutting knife. The vast majority of these novice ramming pilots fell victim to American escort fighters, but at least five or six bombers were rammed.

The brunt of the attack was directed at the 3rd Air Division. The Eighth Air Force INTOPS for the day stated: "Reverting to his old policy of attacking in the area of Dummer and Steinhuder Lakes, the enemy met the leading groups of the first force at 1230 with some 105 to 120 Me 109s, FW 190s and thirty-plus Me 262s, flying between 18,000 and 30,000 feet.

"Of these, only forty-five to fifty single-engined fighters and fifteen jets managed to approach the bombers destroying eleven. ... Enemy aircraft were persistent and continued their attacks as far as Hamburg and Salzwedel, in spite of the beating they were taking."

The fighter escorts claimed sixty-four enemy fighters for the day, and in view of the fact that so few conventional fighters returned to their bases that day, the claims must have been close to accurate. The Mustang pilots only claimed four jets destroyed during the day, and only two of them were confirmed. Just five escorting fighters were lost, and none of these losses were classified as downed by the jets. The 3rd Air Division lost fourteen B-17s.

Captain Verne E. Hooker went after one of two Me 262s that he saw attacking the bombers and scored hits on the jet's left wing. The jet pilot pulled to the left, away from the bombers. Hooker saw two more Me 262s coming in on the bombers from their seven o'clock level position. The Mustang pilot left his original target to go after these two. However, one of the flight leaders in his 435th Fighter Squadron saw the pilot of the aircraft that he had just hit bail out.

Lieutenant Hilton O. Thompson, also from the 479th Fighter Group, was also involved in this combat and was credited with one of the Me 262s.

Lieutenant Richard G. Candelaria of the 479th Group had a very successful day. His first combat took place when he saw two Me 262s come in on the rear of a bomber formation. Candelaria reported: "I came at the leader head-on, trying to make him break, but he avoided my head-on pass by diving, and not altering his course, making it very difficult for me to hit him. I tried to drop my tanks on him, but missed completely. I half-rolled and lined up on his tail as he opened fire on the bombers. I opened fire on the jet, observing hits on both sides of his cockpit, then large puffs of smoke spat from the fuselage and wings.

"In the meantime, the second jet had positioned himself on my tail and opened fire on me. I saw white and red shells, like golf balls, going past me. Looking up into the rear-view mirror, I saw him firing away. A moment later, he hit me in the right wing. Then, the first jet I that had engaged broke away to the left in a lazy half-roll and went straight down, trailing smoke. I broke hard into the jet behind me, but he went off in a shallow dive towards his buddy, going much too fast for me to ever hope to catch."

Lieutenant Floyd W. Salze, in Candelaria's flight reported: "The first jet did a left wing-over and, trailing heavy smoke, went straight down from 17,000 feet into the clouds, which hung at 2,500 to 3,000 feet. The jet was still going straight down when it entered the clouds."

Regardless, Candelaria was credited with a probable for the Me 262. However, he went on that day to destroy four Me 109s, all confirmed.

The 339th Fighter Group skirmished with the jets several times during the day, but it had to settle for one probable, five damaged and another probable that was not credited. Lieutenant Robert V. Blizzard hit one jet during a head-on pass, then peppered another, which went down into the clouds smoking. A chase through the clouds proved futile when the jet could not be located again.

Major Vernon B. Hathorn, Jr., of the 504th Fighter Squadron, was leading the other spare Mustang of the 339th Group when they joined another flight descending to attack Me 262s that were harassing the bombers. The P-51s made several turns, attempting to get on the jets, and Hathorn lost his wingman during these maneuvers. Hathorn joined up with two other Mustangs that were chasing one of the 262s. The pursuit went from 25,000 feet to 10,000 feet, where the jet pilot went into a left turn. For some strange reason, the two Mustangs in front of Hathorn just kept going down.

Hathorn hung onto the jet and finally closed to 200 yards at 5,000 feet. A long burst struck the tail of the 262, which went into a steep right bank. This enabled the P-51 to close further, and Hathorn let go a very long burst, clobbering the craft and igniting its right jet. The enemy plane went down into the clouds at 3,000 feet in a steep spiral. With no witnesses and poor-quality gun camera film, Hathorn received no credit at all.

Later that afternoon, Technical Sergeant Weaver L. Reckland was serving in his usual capacity as engineer gunner in the top turret of the B-17 flown by Lieutenant Eugene V. Yarger, of the 388th Bomb Group. In the vicinity of Oranienburg, Reckland's formation came under attack from Me 262s, one of which he was credited with downing.

He related: "… It was an Me 262, and someone had called to tell me a fighter was coming up fast on us from six o'clock. I was top turret gunner, and we were under heavy fighter attacks. Realizing that, unless he banked under us, he'd have to come up in front of us, I turned my twin .50s around to one o'clock and waited a few seconds. Sure enough, he pulled up in front of us in a steep climb at one o'clock and not more than three or four hundred feet range. …

"It was a dead straight shot. All I had to do was frame him in my sights and pull both triggers, keeping my turret tracking him on up until he trailed smoke and spun down without the pilot ever pulling out. … I think he underestimated his speed and overran us."

The B-24s of the 2nd Air Division were met by about a dozen Me 262s, none of which fell to their guns.

Captain William T. Heily of the 30th Reconnaissance Squadron was shot down by Me 262s from 3/JG 7. Heily was on a photo mission near Seesen when he was attacked by Oberleutnant Walter Schuck, who shot out both the engines of Heily's Lockheed F-4.

Jet action was limited on April 8, as the bombers went after airfields and oil depots. Nine bombers were lost, but these fell to flak. JV 44 reportedly did some flying and lost one aircraft to a P-47. This may have been the victory credited to Lieutenant John J. Usiatynski of the 358th Fighter Group in the vicinity of Nordlingen.

On the morning of April 9, B-24 Liberators of the 2nd Air Division bombed the jet airfields once more. A number of Me 262s were up to intercept, and one of them was downed by Lieutenant James R. Sloan of the 361st Fighter Group. Shortly before target time, he saw an Me 262 making a pass at the bombers.

He reported: "... I fired a short burst, but the Me 262 was out of range and I observed no hits. He destroyed one B-24, and I noticed hits on another while following him to the bombers. My rate of closure was too slow to warrant chasing him, so I climbed to the right to an altitude of 25,000 feet and waited for him to make another pass. When he came in again, I cut him off, split-essed down on him and fired. I did not observe hits, but I had discouraged him from making a pass on the bombers.

"By this time, I did not have any cover and enemy aircraft

Early in its development, Major Wolfgang Spate was one of the primary test pilots on the Me 163. Late in the war, he assumed command of 3/JG 7, and Spate claimed at least five jet victories.

THE MENACE—CLIMAX AND DEMISE

flew all around me. I climbed to 25,000 feet again, cut off another jet making a pass and split-essed ahead on his line of flight. I fired while going down on him, pulled up behind him with a speed of approximately 530 MPH and fired at point-blank range until only one gun was firing. He did not blow up, but when into a slight dive that developed into a spin. He crashed some sixteen miles from the target."

That same morning, Martin B-26 Mauraders from the 387th Bomb Group set out to strike the ordnance depot at Kummersbruck, Germany. As the Mauraders made their bomb run, they were attacked from the rear by Me 262s. The two jets dove down and came in from beneath. On their first pass, the jets shot down the B-26 flown by Lieutenant Stroud, of the 558th Bomb Squadron. The 30 MM fire also struck Lieutenant Frederick Gregg's aircraft, tearing off the rear of the left nacelle and leaving a big hole in the left wing. Fortunately, Gregg was able to make it home.

Major Edward Giller, who was escorting bombers in the vicinity of Munich, saw two Mustangs chasing an Me 262 down below. In view

This line-up of Me 262s belonged to Galland's elite JV 44 unit. Regardless of the number of existing Me 262s, usually only about fifty percent were in commission at any time. (Stigler)

of the fact that he had an altitude advantage, Giller went down after it. The chase went on for about ten minutes, until Giller was down to about 7,000 feet and the jet was at 1,000 feet. The P-51 pilot lost his target for a minute, then spied it trying to get into Munich-Riem Airdrome.

Giller caught it at only fifty feet, right over the perimeter track. Several bursts hit the jet in its left wing and fuselage. Giller noted that the gear was not down on the jet and that it was doing about 200 MPH. Giller was hitting 450 MPH and quickly overran the craft. As he pulled up and looked back, he saw the 262 crash land to the right of the runway, completely wrecking the aircraft.

Later during the day of April 9, Lieutenant Leon M. Orcutt and Lieutenant Harlan E. Hunt, of the 339th Fighter Group, escorted a photo recee F-5 to the Leipzig area. Two Me 262s attempted to break up the mission, but the jets were intercepted by the two Mustangs. Orcutt got on the tail of one as it broke and scored some hits on its right engine, which set it smoking. As he pursued the other jet, it went into a dive from 8,000 feet. Orcutt, who had a rough engine, did not follow.

Hunt went after the second jet and almost collided with it when it pulled up sharply. As the two aircraft pulled up into the sun, Hunt fired blindly, seeing a few strikes. However, the jet continued to pull away from him.

April 10, 1945

April 10, 1945, marked the zenith in the activities of the Luftwaffe jet menace, and to a great extent the events of that day were a powerful factor in its demise. The Eighth Air Force directed more than 1,300 heavy bombers, escorted by more than 900 fighters, against the jet airfields and installations at Brandenburg-Briest, Reichlin-Larz, Oranienburg, Neuruppin, Burg and Parchim. The force was so overwhelming that several of the fighter units were sent out as free-lancers looking for opposition.

The badly depleted Luftwaffe was able to put up only a dozen Focke Wulf 190 Ds and fifty-five Me 262s to intercept the invaders. The first force, composed of 442 B-17s from the 1st Air Division, targeted the airfield and army headquarters at Oranienburg. This force encountered thirty to forty Me 262s.

The jets were not able to break through the escort to make mass attacks, but instead came in singly or in small flights from five to seven o'clock, low or level, usually making only one pass before breaking away. The first force lost at least five B-17s before the jets were driven off by the escort at great cost to the Me 262s.

The second force, consisting of 144 B-17s from the 3rd Air Division, bombed the airfield at Neuruppin. Although they encountered no enemy aircraft, they lost one Fortress to flak.

The third force, which included 372 B-17s from the 3rd Air Division, bombed Zerbst Airfield, Brandenburg-Briest Airfield and Burg-Magdeburg Airfield. Ten Me 262s intercepted and managed to down five of the B-17s, while three were lost to flak.

The fourth force, composed of 357 B-24s from the 2nd Air Division, sortied against Rechlin Airfield, Parchim Airfield and Rechlin-Larz Airfield. The Liberators encountered no enemy air opposition and lost only one aircraft to flak.

One of the lead units that was escorting the bombers that afternoon was the 20th Fighter Group. Captain John K. Hollins, of the 79th Fighter Squadron, was leading two flights that were out on a sweep in front of the bomber stream. Hollins was in the vicinity of Parchim Airfield when he sighted some of the first Me 262s getting airborne. "We were at 6,000 feet. … We saw two Me 262s at 2,000 feet, flying at us from eleven o'clock, a half mile away, in a slight climb. I split-essed, dropped my tanks, gave my plane full-throttle and headed straight for the ground in a sixty-degree dive, which put me directly on the tail of an enemy aircraft at about 2,000 feet. I gave him a four-second burst from 200 yards away, dead astern. My speed was roughly 500 MPH. … The jet was definitely using power in a gentle climb. My burst evidently hit in the center of the fuselage as the enemy aircraft exploded. ... The other jet avoided us with great speed."

Captain John K. Brown, of the 20th Group's 55th Fighter Squadron, was leading Red Flight when six Me 262s attempted to jump the bombers just after they came off their target. The jets were flying in pairs, and when challenged, they split. Brown took off after one that had split to the left, and it swung around in a big circle. Brown saw tracers from the bombers going by his canopy, so he pulled closer to the jet.

The 262 tried to turn with him, which enabled Brown to open fire with a thirty-degree deflection shot from 400 yards. The .50-caliber bullets struck home and large hunks flew off the jet. Brown hung on and hit the 262 again. It split-essed and went straight down from 7,000 feet. The enemy craft was seen to hit the ground and explode.

The 77th Fighter Squadron, of the 20th Group, also engaged the jets when they attempted to attack the bombers. The Yellow Flight chased two of the Me 262s that had attempted to come in on the Fortresses from their six o'clock. The enemy fled at high speed, and the P-51s finally gave up pursuit. Lieutenant John W. Cudd, Jr., joined up with Flight Officer Jerome Rosenblum as they headed back toward the bombers. En route, they met an Me 262 coming toward them in a dive from one o'clock.

It appeared that he intended to make a head-on pass, but he broke short and wound up with both Mustangs turning inside of him. Cudd fired several bursts, hitting the jet in the fuselage and wing roots. Rosenblum then hit it in the cockpit, and the Me 262 went into a dive, then pulled up in a climb. The canopy flew off, and the jet went back into a dive from which it did not recover. The pilot did not get out.

Lieutenant Albert B. North, also from the 77th Fighter Squadron, and his flight also pursued Me 262s after they tried to get through to the B-17s. Once more, the enemy outdistanced the Mustangs at high speed. When North came back to the bombers at 25,000 feet, he happened upon a lone Me 262 closing on the rear of the bomber formation. North closed on him and opened fire from 50 yards dead astern. The jet nosed over and went straight down into the ground.

Lieutenant Walter T. Drozd, of the 77th Fighter Squadron, scored the 20th Group's fifth confirmed victory of the day. Drozd and his element leader took off after an Me 262 in another of the day's futile pursuits. On their return to the bomber stream, they too, were lucky enough to find a victim.

They spotted an Me 262 down low, which obviously did not see them. The two Mustangs went down at high speed, and Drozd's element leader overshot the jet just as he began to fire. Drozd opened fire and stitched his bullets into the jet before he overshot as well. The jet dropped its landing gear and crashed into the ground burning.

Captain Gordon B. Compton was leading Red Flight in the 353rd Fighter Group's 351st Fighter Squadron on their escort mission, when jets were reported to the south, flying in the area of Dessau.

An Me 262 is apparently parked on a taxiway leading into a forest. Late in the war, many Luftwaffe aircraft operated from highways and were hidden away in the trees. (via Ethell)

After a few turns and orbits of the area, Compton picked up an Me 262 flying right down on the deck. The P-51 pilot went into a dive from 10,000 feet and had pulled up on the side of the enemy aircraft before the jet pilot was aware of him. Compton slid over on its tail and opened fire. The aircraft began to burn and crashed on Kothen Airdrome.

Captain Robert W. Abernathy of the 353rd Group's 350th Fighter Squadron was circling the bombers' target, when a bogie was called out at seven o'clock high. The Mustangs finished a turn to the left and an Me 262 turned right, putting the P-51s on its rear. The jet sped away and was nearly lost from sight. Suddenly, it made the usual fatal mistake of taking a wide sweeping turn when the enemy was looking. By the time it had made a 180-degree turn, Abernathy had him head-on. A long-range shot struck home, and flames roared out of the engine nacelles. The pilot bailed out.

Lieutenant Jack W. Clark and Lieutenant Bruce D. Memahan from the 350th Fighter Squadron caught an Me 262 down on the deck over the city of Dessau. The jet pilot was apparently tooling along at low speed, and the Mustangs were on him before he was aware of their presence. Clark's fire hit the jet's left wing and engine, while McMahan hit its right wing and engine. The Luftwaffe pilot pulled up in a steep climb and bailed out.

Two pilots from the 359th Fighter Group were successful over Gardelegen Airdrome. Lieutenant Harold Tenenbaum was flying at 14,000 feet, when the bombers came under attack from Me 262s. He was driven out of the area by heavy flak, but at 16,000 feet, he spotted an Me 262 being chased by two Mustangs down below. Tenenbaum went down to join the chase, but the jet quickly sped away from the area. Tenenbaum then saw two planes down on the deck, so he dove down from 8,000 feet to 1,000 feet.

The two planes turned out to be P-51s chasing an Me 262 that was far out of their range. With his diving speed, Tenenbaum was able to pull into range of the jet, and he opened fire from 300 yards, then pulled right on around on its tail.

The jet pilot dropped his gear and began his attempt to land on the airfield. Tenenbaum continued to close and fire, peppering the aircraft. Pieces of the aircraft flew off and the right engine disintegrated into flames. Tenenbaum was driven off by intense flak, but the 262 hit the field burning and skidded onto another field where it blew up.

Tenenbaum climbed back up and orbited the field in hopes that he could catch another jet coming in to land. He finally sighted one and dove on him, but the jet sped away, and after a five-minute chase, Tenenbaum cut him off in a turn.

However, the Luftwaffe pilot increased his speed and headed for Gardelegen Airdrome with the Mustang 800 yards behind and firing away. Tenenbaum was forced to break off the chase due to heavy light flak, and by the time he could close once more, the jet had already landed safely.

Lieutenant Robert J. Guggenos, the second pilot from the 369th Fighter Squadron to score that day, peeled off and attacked an Me 262 as it came in to land on Gardelegen Airdrome. The Luftwaffe pilot's aircraft was apparently out of fuel; he used no evasive action when the Mustang pulled up on his tail and opened fire with a long burst. The jet lit up all over, went into a steep glide, then crashed and burned.

The one Thunderbolt victory that day was won when Lieutenant Walter J. Sharbo, of the 56th Fighter Group's 62nd Squadron, dove on an unsuspecting Me 262 down below and blasted him from 600 yards. The jet's canopy came off, and the aircraft plunged into Muritz Lake from 1,500 feet.

One flight from the 4th Fighter Group's 336th Fighter Squadron went down after an Me 262 that was maneuvering into position to make a pass on some of the 56th Group's Thunderbolts. As the flight descended, the flight leader fired. When he did so, the 262 turned directly in front of Lieutenant Wilmer W. Collins, who delivered a long burst into the jet. The jet descended through the clouds to the deck with the Mustang right behind. Following another burst, the 262 hit some trees and spun in.

Lieutenant Keith R. McGinnis, of the 55th Fighter Group's 38th Fighter Squadron, witnessed a maneuver that had first became prevalent in the fall of 1944: Upon engagement with an Allied aircraft, novice Luftwaffe pilots often immediately bailed out without enemy fire. At this point during the war, novice pilots were manning some of the Me 262s in jet units.

McGinnis and his flight had sighted two Me 262s approaching the bombers, but by the time the Mustang pilots had dumped their tanks and dropped down on the enemy craft, the jets were already under and attacking the bombers. As McGinnis closed on one of the Me 262s and maneuvered into range, the pilot half-rolled and bailed out.

Lieutenant Colonel Earl D. Duncan was leading the 328th Fighter Squadron, of the 352nd Fighter Group, when their bomber formation was intercepted by eight Me 262s. After their initial passes, some of the jets tried to make passes at lower speeds, enabling the escorts to close on them. Duncan and his wingman, Major Richard G. McAuliffe, went after one of the jets and managed to box it in down on the deck.

Duncan fired a two-second burst from astern at 250 yards, and the Luftwaffe pilot jettisoned his canopy and pulled straight up. Duncan attempted to follow, but overran it, while McAuliffe hit the craft with a effective burst as the jet stalled off to the right. The pilot bailed out, but his parachute never opened.

Lieutenant Charles C. Pattilo, of the 352nd's 487th Fighter Squadron, chased one Me 262, which had been flying south of Ulzen for about ten minutes. The jet finally began to let down in an attempt to land. Pattilo easily pulled into range and began to fire short bursts, without signs of success. Two other Mustangs made one pass from above, firing, but one of the jet's engines burst into flames, and it slammed into the airfield.

THE MENACE—CLIMAX AND DEMISE

Lieutenants Joseph W. Prichard and Carlo A. Ricci, of the 487th Fighter Squadron, teamed up to down one of the Me 262s that had made a pass on their bomber formation. They joined to chase after the jet, which faked a turn to the right but turned left after Prichard fired on it. When it turned left, Ricci, who was on the tail end of the chase, was able to cut in and open fire. The 262 pilot pulled up several hundred feet in a zoom, and the pilot bailed out. His parachute opened just before he hit the ground.

Lieutenant Kenneth A. Lashbrook, of the 55th Fighter Group's 338th Fighter Squadron, was credited with the destruction of an Me 262 without firing a shot. He and his flight had been making strafing runs on the airfield at Burg, and he became separated from the rest. As he emerged from the smoke and dust that billowed right down on the deck, several P-51s chased a lone Me 262 across his path, flying about 100 feet above his Mustang.

The enemy pilot was staying out of the range of the other P-51s and apparently did not see Lashbrook until he was about 300 yards away. When the jet pilot did see the Mustang, he attempted a frantic turn to the right, snapped over on his back and went straight into a canal.

Lieutenant Wayne C. Gatlin, of the 360th Fighter Squadron, of the 356th Fighter Group, caught an Me 262 making an overhead pass at the bombers from six o'clock. As the jet hit a straggler and continued in its dive, Gatlin wound up on its tail. A long burst from 200 yards struck the enemy craft, which continued in its dive until it struck the ground.

Pilots of the 364th Fighter Group had escorted the bombers to Oranienburg where they, too, met with Me 262s. Captain Douglas J. Pick and Lieutenant Harry C. Schwarz shared in the destruction of one jet. The bogie was called out by Schwartz, so Pick told him to go after it. He did so in short order and managed to score some good hits on the jet, which rolled over and looked as if it would crash momentarily.

The No. 4 man in the formation then took a shot as he passed, and Pick rolled over, waiting to see the 262 crash. However, the jet straightened up. Immediately, Pick opened fire, and the nose of the 262 dropped as it crashed in a ball of fire.

For the men in the bombers, it had been a hectic day. As usual, the 100th Bomb Group was in the middle of the action. As one crewmember recalled: "The jets made several passes at us from six o'clock low. I distinctly remember two ships going down in flames. Lieutenant Delbert Reeves, who was on his first mission, was flying in my squadron in front of me and a little higher; his bomber burst into flames and a wing was ripped off during one of the first jet passes." Of the nine men aboard Reeves's aircraft, only the bombardier was able to get out.

The Fortress flown by Lieutenant Lawrence Bazin was forced to leave formation with its No. 2 engine feathered. As it tried to get back in formation, an Me 262 hit knocked pieces off the bomber's right wing. No. 3 and 4 engines then burst into flames, and the plane went down. Both pilots, plus the ball turret and tail gunner, were killed. The rest of the crew bailed out, to become prisoners of war.

Staff Sergeant Les Lind, a ball turret gunner in the 379th Bomb Group, recalled: "Two jets made a diving attack on our squadron from five and seven o'clock high. I caught a glimpse of the one that came in from seven o'clock as it pulled out of its dive, and I gave it a good burst from my twin fifties. I will never, never forget that sight. There was this big jet with its black crosses on the undersides of its wings, and my tracer bullets going right into its belly. I kept hearing the tail gunner's guns firing as long as he could keep the jet in his sights. He abruptly yelled, 'Holy shit! Two P-51s just came down on him and blew him out of the sky.' … The jet that had come in from five o'clock had knocked down the Fortress on our right wing. … The stricken Fort started to fall on its right wing with its entire vertical tail fin shot off! The jets' attacks continued, and one of the ships in the lead squadron was clobbered."

"Finally, a fanatical pilot came in at us from seven o'clock level, flying through a hail of bullets that came from every top turret, ball turret and tail gun in our formation. I started firing at him when he was about a thousand yards away and didn't stop until my right gun jammed just as he swooshed by us at nine o'clock level. We knew that he had been hit because black smoke was trailing him. After he had gone past our squadron, two Mustangs jumped him and finished him off."

The 303rd Bomb Group fought the jets for about twenty minutes after coming off their target at Oranienbug. *Henn's Revenge,* flown by Lieutenant R.L. Murray, was hit by Me 262s coming in on its tail. It burst into flames between No. 3 and No. 4 engines and went down out of control. The top turret gunner was the only survivor.

Luftwaffe losses were tragic. The base at Burg was completely destroyed, including a dozen Me 262s that had been caught on the ground. Parchim was not damaged nearly as bad due to weather conditions that had caused the brunt of the bombs to miss the target.

However, JG 7 lost twenty-seven Me 262s, which was fifty percent of its strength. At least five pilots were known dead, with eight surviving to fight again. The balance were missing, either dead or prisoners. One great pilot loss was the Knights Cross-winner Oberleutenant Franz Schall, who was one of the more successful pilots in Nowotny's Kommando and was Staffelkapitan of 10/JG. Schall had downed a Mustang in combat and was attempting to land at Parchim when his Me 262 hit a bomb crater and exploded. Schall was credited with sixteen victories while flying the Me 262, in addition to the 117 victories he had scored on the Eastern Front.

That night, orders came for JG 7 to move to bases at Plattling, Muhldorf, Landau and Prague/Ruzyen. At Prague/Ruzyen, they would be joined by KG (J) 54.

APRIL 11 AND 14, 1945

On the eleventh, the only confirmed action by the U.S. Army Air

Force with a German jet was that of Lieutenant Benjamin Hall, III, of the 52nd Fighter Group's 2nd Fighter Squadron. Hall came upon an Arado 234 in the Bologna area of Italy. The P-51 pilot pulled in on the jet and set its left engine aflame. The 234 went into a gentle dive from 22,000 feet and never recovered.

The next jet combats with positive results did not occur until April 14. Both of these encounters involved pilots from the 354th Fighter Group, of the Ninth Air Force. During the first encounter, Captain Clayton K. Gross, of the 355th Fighter Squadron, was leading a flight of four Mustangs along the Elbe River south of Berlin looking for enemy fighters. Just south of the river while flying at 12,000 feet, Gross spotted an airfield, and as he gave it his concentrated attention, he spotted an Me 262 circling at 2,000 feet.

Gross recalls the incident: "I knew full well what they [Me 262s] were capable of by now, but with surprise and 10,000 feet, I felt I had a good chance at the one below me. I rolled over and pulled the stick back to start nearly straight down. To help, I left power on.

"My eyes were on my unsuspecting victim, but I stole a glance at the airspeed indicator in time to see it at 450 and

Oberleutnant Franz Schall became a fifty-plus victory ace on the Eastern Front before he joined Major Nowotny in September, 1944. He scored at least sixteen victories in the Me 262 before he was killed attempting to land on April 10, 1945.

THE MENACE—CLIMAX AND DEMISE

still winding up. Suddenly, I lost all interest in the jet as my control stick began to feel loose and quickly felt like nothing—as if it had suddenly disconnected. I kicked-pushed-pulled everything I had—still nothing. At that instant, I felt slight resistance on the stick. I tried easing back slightly. I was gradually pulling out.

"Now guess what? The original object of my attention was absolutely dead ahead of me, and I was closing rapidly. ... My initial burst set its left jet burning and a fairly large section of his left wingtip flew off, causing me to flinch as it went past me. The speed of my dive caused me to overrun him, and I pulled off right and up to lose speed, then rolled back to reposition myself.

"... When I rolled back on his tail again, I found the pilot standing the Me 262 on end and climbing straight up! And accelerating as he did it. I tried to follow with some of my remaining diving speed and full-power, but Mustangs won't fly in that direction very long. With his left jet still burning, he was pulling away! ... Then something happened to his power. He slowed—still going straight up—then stopped and began to slide back downhill, tail first. As it started to fall off, the pilot ejected. I had a jet!

"The pilot's chute popped open, and I temporarily forgot the airdrome we were over—forgot it that is until every flak gun on the field opened up at me. My flight was now catching up. ... When the flak started, we busted ass to get out of there."

Fifty years later, Gross would meet his victim, Kurt Lobgensang, who was a 19-year-old member of 1/JG 7 at the time.

The second victory scored by a 354th Group pilot came that afternoon, when Lieutenant Loyd Overfield of the 353rd Fighter Squadron led a formation to the Riesa area. They observed three Me 262s headed south of Riesa. Another Me 262 was seen coming up behind the Mustangs, and one of the pilots got on its tail but lost it in the clouds.

Overfield shot down an He 111 near Dresden, then returned to

Riesa where he made a diving attack on an Me 262. Overfield hit it with several bursts, and the jet exploded as the pilot bailed out.

General Adolf Galland and Me 262s from JV 44 were out and hunting on April 16. Galland and some of his charges intercepted a formation of Ninth Air Force B-26s, and he claimed two of them shot down. It is possible that his victims came from the 322nd Bomb Group, which lost two Marauders that day.

That afternoon, a dozen Thunderbolts from the Ninth Air Force's 368th Fighter Group caught some Me 262s taking off from an airfield west of Prague, Czechoslovakia. Lieutenants Henry A. Yandel and Vernon E. Fein were each credited with the destruction of one of the aircraft.

Major Eugene E. Ryan, of the 55th Fighter Group's 338th Fighter Squadron, was leading his squadron in the vicinity of Linz, Austria, when a bogie was called in down on the deck. Ryan came down from 5,000 feet and noted an Me 262 making a long approach to an airfield.

As Ryan closed in for the kill, a red flare was shot up from the airfield. With this warning, the pilot chose to

Captain Clayton K. Gross, of the 354th Fighter Group, attacked and downed an Me 262 in the Weimer area on April 14, 1945. (Gross)

belly the jet in just short of the airfield, where it struck a grove of tall trees. When the P-51s pulled up, they noted smoke rising to 300 feet.

APRIL 17, 1945

Action increased on April 17, when most of the Eighth Air Force heavy bombers were targeting Dresden. Both JV 44 and JG 7 were in action and they flew a number of attacks against the bombers. JV 44 attacked the 305th Bomb Group. Unteroffizier Edward Schallmoser made his pass, but he was caught in a crossfire from the bombers' gunners and hit. His jet collided with the No. 3 plane in the high squadron, cutting off the tail unit of the Fortress. Lieutenant Branard H. Harris and all of his crew were lost.

Amazingly, Schallmoser survived the collision. He managed to bail out of his badly damaged Me 262 and make it back to base in relatively good condition.

Lieutenant John C. Campbell, Jr., of the 339th Fighter Group's 503rd Fighter Squadron, joined a chase after an Me 262 that had made a pass at the bombers, but they were soon outdistanced. As the Mustangs were about to give up, another Me 262 crossed over in front of them.

Lieutenant Joseph G. Farrell and his wingman initially went after the jet, but they overshot. Campbell pulled six Gs and managed to follow the 262 down to the deck, firing away. He got good strikes on the left jet engine. The 262 pilot made a turn to the right and levelled off at 200 feet. The Mustang pilot then shot chunks off the jet's left wing and walked his fire into the fuselage. The pilot bailed out, but his parachute did not open.

Captain Roy W. Orndorff led the 383rd Fighter Squadron, of the 364th Fighter Group, while escorting the bombers, and they encountered Me 262s in the Prague area. Orndorff managed to down one of the jets, while members of his squadron accounted for two more.

Captain Walter L. Goff chased one of the jets that had intercepted the bombers, but finally lost it in the haze. Goff returned to the Pilsen area and found an airfield, where he set up an orbiting vigil at about 3,000 feet. Shortly thereafter, an Me 262 appeared 1,000 feet below. As soon as Goff turned towards it, the jet pilot made a pass over the airfield.

The Mustang pilot went right after him and opened fire. The Luftwaffe pilot pulled straight up and Goff scored heavily on the jet's left wing and left engine. At about 2,000 feet, the jet slowly rolled to the left with the P-51 right behind, still firing short bursts. The 262 caught fire, and the pilot bailed out.

Lieutenant William F. Kissel also chased an Me 262, destroying it when the Luftwaffe pilot attempted a landing. Kissel fired at it from three o'clock, and as he passed over the jet, he observed it dig one wing into the ground. Captain George Varner saw a plane slide down the field and blow up, but could not identify it positively as the one that Kissel had fired at, so it went in the books as a probable.

Kissel and Varner continued on and caught some Me 262s at Falkenst airfield. Two Me 262s were pulling off the side of the strip, one was still on the strip and a fourth Me 262 was making an approach for landing. Varner hit the jet sitting on the end of the strip and set it afire. Kissel came in astern of the 262 that was coming in on its final approach. A long burst hit the jet when it was about half-way down the strip, and it blew up.

The 357th Fighter Group also got into some Me 262s in the area of Prague, and once more, a chase after one enemy aircraft turned up a second. Flight Officer James A. Steiger spotted a jet, flying at 6,000 feet headed north, on the east side of Prague. Steiger tried to turn inside the craft, but this time the jet turned inside the P-51.

Steiger pulled up in a wing-over and rolled out on the tail of the 262. He fired from 600 yards until he was at point-blank range. The jet fell off on its left wing and slammed into the ground.

The Ninth Air Force also saw considerable action against the jets during the day. Lieutenant James A. Zweizig, of the 371st Fighter Group's 404th Fighter Squadron, caught an Me 262 as it was taking off from an airdrome near Eger and downed it.

Captain Jack A. Warner, of the 353rd Fighter Squadron, of the 354th Fighter Group, was leading eight Mustangs on a mission near Karlsbad. His flight was flying top cover for another flight of P-51s that was shooting up motor transport.

Warner spied an Me 262 down around 1,500 feet and went down after it. As he closed, the jet pilot began to throttle forward. However, before the jet could escape, Warner hit the aircraft in its fuselage, right wing and right engine. After that, the jet lost speed and went into a slight dive. Warner continued to fire and score hits in its left engine. The aircraft just continued to dive until it crashed through some trees and into a hill.

B-26 Marauders from the 17th Bomb Group, based at Dijon, France, attacked the Dettelsau ammunition dump, and as they approached the target area, they came under attack from six Me 262s. One of the Marauders was damaged, and Staff Sergeant James A. Valimont, tail gunner on one of the B-26s, was severely wounded when the tail of his craft was hit by 30 MM fire.

Valimont, however, drug himself back to his guns despite his wounds, and when the Me 262 made a second pass on his aircraft, he damaged the jet to the extent that it was forced to break off its onslaught and dive away.

APRIL 18, 1945

Both JG 7 and JV 44 were active on April 18, and the first jet action of the day took place during the morning while the 356th Fighter Group was escorting Ninth Air Force B-26s. The target was north of Augsburg, which was bombed without aerial opposition.

As the Mustangs came off the target, a bogie was sighted at twelve o'clock high. Green Flight from the 359th Fighter Squadron asked for permission to identify, and when it was granted, they began their climb from 10,000 feet toward the bogie at 12,000 feet. Green Leader announced it was a jet, so he and his wingman went after the aircraft, which was now in a shallow dive. Green Leader made one attack and fired, but for some reason broke off the attack.

Lieutenant Leon Oliver, who was flying Green Three reported: "After Green Leader broke off his attack, the enemy aircraft pulled out of its dive and started to climb, flying toward the southeast. I passed through the first element, pulling up behind the enemy during its climb and recognized it as a Jerry jet [an Arado 234]. I figured the jet would pull away in the climb, so I started to fire at it from 700 to 900 yards, dead astern. I scored no hits with the first two or three bursts.

"As I was closing, I decided to hold my fire until I was in good range, and I gave him another burst from 300 to 400 yards without deflection—again, no hits. The enemy aircraft leveled off, and I gave it another burst, scoring hits on its left wing tip. It then appeared that my sight and range were okay, so I really let him have it, scoring hits on his left wing and left jet unit.

"By this time, I could see holes in the rear of its jet units and could smell the odor of burning low-grade fuel. The enemy aircraft started a shallow turn to the left. I continued to close and kept firing, seeing strikes move across the left wing into the fuselage and right wing. I then pulled my sight back to the left and kept working on the left jet, which was smoking profusely from a small visible fire. I put the sight in the middle of the smoke and let him have it. … As I overran it, the enemy aircraft went into a spin. I was then at 13,000 to 14,000 feet, but I saw him spin into the ground, hitting between two houses and exploding and burning."

When the Eighth Air Force bombers headed for rail targets in Germany, Me 262s from JV 44 began to get airborne. As Knights Cross winner Oberst Johannes Steinhoff began his take off, he suffered a flameout on one of his engines.

The aircraft began to settle, then it struck the ground, leaving a stream of fire behind. The landing gear was ripped off, and the jet skidded to a stop in a mass of flames. Miraculously, a severely burned Steinhoff staggered out from the wreckage. Many months of recovery were before him, but he later would become a general in the West German Air Force.

Major Don Bochkay was leading a flight in the 357th Fighter Group's 363rd Fighter Squadron, when he spotted an Me 262 in the target area southwest of Praha, Czechoslovakia. Bochkay went down from 15,000 to 13,000 feet and apparently pulled in on the tail of the jet unseen. He caught the craft with a good burst from 400 yards and saw strikes on the right engine and canopy.

Immediately, the Luftwaffe pilot broke hard right in a diving turn, pulling streamers from his wingtips. Bochkay turned with him and latched onto him once more at 7,000 feet. Another outpouring of .50-caliber slugs tore once again into the right engine, and the pilot jettisoned his canopy. Further bursts caused the aircraft to break up in mid-air. Finally, the tail section tore off, and the jet rolled over and went down like a torch.

Captain Charles E. Weaver of the 357th Group's 362nd Fighter Squadron attacked the airfield at Prague/Ruzney. Weaver related: "I spotted a lone Me 262 at one o'clock low to us, coming head-on. We dropped tanks and split-essed to the jet, which took cover in the clouds. Almost immediately, I sighted three Me 262s at one o'clock , spiralling down over the field to make landings.

"I took chase and fired a three-second burst at maximum range; my target was tail-end Charlie. I closed further, cutting him off in the turn, to about 500 yards, almost dead astern, continuing to fire. Our altitude was 5,000 feet.

"My ammunition was almost expended, so I tried to close further before firing again, when he almost stopped in mid-air. I pulled up sharply to avoid over-shooting. Upon recovering sight of him, I found that he was directly beneath me in a flat spin to the left. I saw the pilot bail out, but did not see his chute open. Our encounter had taken us through considerable flak, and my wingman called out that he had been hit. Soon afterwards, he was forced to bail out, but his chute opened successfully."

Several other Me 262s were damaged near the airfield, with the 357th Group hitting four of them. Major Leonard K. Carson damaged two.

Lieutenant Colonel Dale E. Shafer, Jr., of the 339th Fighter Group, downed an Arado 234 in the vicinity of Regensburg. His group had just made rendezvous with the bombers, when he saw the enemy aircraft 3,000 feet below. The Arado was at eight o'clock and traveling in the same direction as the Mustangs. Shafer broke to the left and took off after it. The Luftwaffe pilot banked left and went into a rather steep climb as the P-51 pilot closed on him.

Shafer fired one short burst from maximum range but saw no strikes. He continued to close, peppering the jet with short bursts, which began to rip into the 234. When the distance was down to 200 yards, white smoke began to stream from the right engine and a fire broke out. The pilot jettisoned his canopy, at about 12,000 feet, but he didn't jump until he was down around 3,000 feet. Shortly thereafter, the aircraft exploded and the fragments scattered into a forest.

Mustangs from the Fifteenth Air Force were out looking for jets and shooting up their airfields. Major Ralph F. Johnson, Commanding Officer of the 325th Fighter Group's 318th Fighter Squadron, caught an Me 262 on takeoff and went down after it. He ripped the jet with his fire until it rolled over on its back and went in.

Twice during the day, B-26s from the 322nd Bomb Group were attacked by Me 262s, but in neither case did they lose aircraft. Three of the Marauders were damaged, while their gunners managed to hit a couple of the jets.

THE MENACE—CLIMAX AND DEMISE

April 19 marked the last day that American fighters would encounter jets from JG 7 in the air, and it also marked the last day that the jets would be met in any numbers by the Eighth Air Force bombers. That day, the bombers set out to bomb rail targets, primarily in the Prague, Czechoslovakia, and Dresden, Germany, areas.

Leading the A Group, of the 357th Fighter Group, was Lieutenant Colonel Jack W. Hayes, Jr., who reported: "I assigned Greenhouse Squadron [364th] ... to the first box [of bombers], assigned Dollar Squadron [362nd] to the second box and swept ahead of both sides of the first box with my Cement Squadron [363rd]. Approximately sixty miles west of Prague, and about four minutes before the bombers turned on a heading of 23 degrees toward the Initial Point, I took up a heading toward the jet airfield at Prague, figuring that enemy opposition would probably come from that area. I arrived at Prague/Ruzyne Airfield at approximately 1149, at an altitude of 23,000 feet.

"There was no activity on the field at this time, so I made one orbit up sun. Upon completing this orbit, I observed an Me 262 taxiing near one of the runways, and immediately after, a two-ship element took off. I started letting down and instructed the squadron to let some more enemy aircraft take off before making a bounce.

"When approximately fourteen jet aircraft had become airborne, I gave the order to drop tanks and get after them. Two flights had dropped tanks just prior to this. I picked out two Me 262s that were just starting a take-off run and circled above them, letting down, making my bounce when they were abut 2,000 feet west of the field in a shallow left turn.

"They were moving comparatively slowly, and I chopped throttle and lowered flaps to keep from overrunning. As soon as I opened fire, the element leader broke left, and his No. 2 man broke right. I followed the leader in a turn to the left and observed strikes on the fuselage as he rolled out in an easterly heading.

GERMAN JETS VS. THE U.S. ARMY AIR FORCE

"The enemy aircraft then hit the deck and turned on the power, and I followed with full power. I dropped into his slipstream and was out of control temporarily, observing my fire falling short. We crossed the river running south out of Prague, and as I reached the western bank, I encountered intense and accurate ground fire, which continued across the river.

"I hit the deck and observed tracers coming over both wings and many hits in the water all around me. The Me 262 flew out of sight behind a tall building on the eastern shore of the river. As I pulled up over this building, I saw him hit the ground in a turn to the right. He dove in at about 30-degrees into a cleared area and blew up—the burning remains slid into a building.

"I then observed another Me 262 at about two o'clock high, heading northeast. As I pulled up after him, I cleared my tail and glimpsed a plane behind me. I took it for granted that it was my wingman, as I had called him just as I made my bounce and he was with me then. However, as I looked back at the jet ahead, my wingman called and said he had lost me. I immediately cleared my tail again and identified the pursuing aircraft as an Me 262. Identification was considerably simplified by the fact that he was firing at me with everything he had. I broke right and up, the jet followed me for about 90 degrees, then it turned to the left. I completed my turn and chased him to the deck, but he easily outdistanced me."

Three more jets were destroyed during the course of this attack on the airfield. One of the busiest Mustang pilots that day was Lieutenant Robert S. Fifield. He took his flight down from 16,000 feet and latched onto one of the 262s that had just taken off, which had gotten about three miles away from its base.

Fifield opened fire when in range and continued to blast away until he overran his target. He pulled the nose of his Mustang up and dropped back down on the tail of the jet, which he continued to pepper until its left engine caught fire. The craft rolled over on its back, went straight in and exploded.

Fifield pulled back up from 2,000 feet, seeking company from his fellow P-51 pilots. Flying at about 10,000 feet, he sighted another Me 262 down below and went down to attack, but he was driven off by light flak from the airfield.

Fifield then joined up with Lieutenant Glenwood A. Zarnke to help protect some stragglers from the bomber formation that were coming under attack from jets. The two Mustangs went down and drove off one Me 262 that had been attacking a straggler. Fifield turned inside the enemy aircraft and got off a couple of bursts, but he missed.

He then attempted to get Zarnke in position to attack the jet, which was leading them a merry chase and attempting to get back to his airfield. Zarnke finally maneuvered into position to fire and emptied his guns at the enemy plane, but he never could close enough to get good results.

Lieutenant Paul Bowles was in on the initial attack at Prague/Ruzyne Airfield, and had scored a few hits on an Me 262 that had just gotten airborne. The jet, however, quickly outdistanced him. He pulled back up, keeping the enemy aircraft in sight, and when it attempted to get back to the airfield, he dove down on it and scored more hits on its wings and fuselage.

Both aircraft were down at treetop level, when the Me 262 went into a left turn. The Mustang pilot began to turn inside of the jet, when he saw it suddenly plunge into the ground and explode.

Lieutenant Carroll W. Ofsthun had followed his flight leader down in a dive when the airfield attack began. As the Mustangs were pursuing one of the Me 262s, Ofsthun saw another jet pass beneath him, flying ninety degrees to his left. Ofsthun immediately went into a wing-over and lined up behind the Me 262. A short burst scored heavily in the cockpit area, and the jet slammed into the ground and disintegrated into flames.

The 357th B Group encountered two Me 262s in the target area that were attacking the bombers and proceeded to give chase. Captain Ivan L. McGuire and Lieutenant Gilman L. Weber kept cutting one of the jets off as it attempted to break through to the bombers. Both the Mustang pilots scored hits on the Me 262, which finally broke off its attacks and made a run for its airfield northwest of Prague. The jet pilot didn't quite make it and bellied in as he neared the field.

Lieutenant James P. McMullen had joined McGuire and Weber in the chase, and as they neared the Prague/Ruzyen Airdrome, Weber called out another Me 262 down below. McMullen went into a steep wing-over and came in on the tail of the jet at about 3,000 feet. After a series of short bursts, the right engine of the enemy aircraft was blazing. The enemy pilot bailed out.

It had been an outstanding day for the 357th Fighter Group, with six Me 262s destroyed.

One other victory over an Me 262 was scored during the day; Lieutenant Robert DeLoach of the 55th Fighter Group's 338th Fighter Squadron. DeLoach was involved in a fifteen-minute chase of an Me 262 before he told his leader that he was taking his flight down to check traffic at the airfields in the vicinity of Prague. As he let down, he received a call on the radio informing him that an Me 262 was attacking his flight from seven o'clock.

DeLoach broke and saw the jet coming in about 1,000 feet behind another flight of Mustangs. As he approached the Me 262, they met head-on. A two-second burst from the guns of the Mustang scored hits on the left engine of the jet, which began to burn. The Luftwaffe pilot went down twisting and turning, but its engine continued to flame. The enemy pilot attempted to belly his aircraft in, but it exploded as he touched down.

Five B-17s, four from the 490th Bomb Group and one from the 447th Bomb Group, fell under the lethal 30 MM guns of the Me 262s. The most successful attack was made by two Me 262s that came in from eight o'clock low on the 490th Group and passed through the low squadron. They then attacked the high squadron and destroyed three Fortresses.

Two B-26 Marauder bomb groups were also attacked by Me 262s during the day. The 322nd came under attack by about ten jets at 1620 hours, after it had bombed the Donauworth railroad bridge.

The jets made passes from the rear, which continued for some minutes before the Thunderbolts of the 404th Fighter Group arrived to break things up. Two B-26s were damaged, while two Me 262s were damaged by gunners on the bombers, and a third was hit by one of the P-47 pilots. Earlier in the day, the 394th Bomb Group was attacked without losses.

APRIL 20, 1945

On April 20, the B-26 Marauders of the 323rd Bomb Group experienced sharp action with a group of Me 262s during a mission to Memmingen. Just as the bombers turned at the Initial Point to begin their bomb run, they were hit from the rear.

The B-26 flown by Lieutenant Dale E. Sanders was struck in the left engine. Flames began to billow from the engine and the bombardier immediately salvoed the bombs. The Marauder fell out of formation and started down.

Several tail gunners on the bombers under attack let loose with their .50-calibers, as did a few of the top turret gunners who were able to bring their guns to bear. Sergeant Edward S. Tyskiewicz let loose a long burst that ripped into one of the Me 262s, and the jet exploded. Tyskiewicz's aircraft was hit, and he was painfully wounded.

Lieutenant Jim Vining was flying in the rear formation of the 323rd, when Me 262s came in from the six o'clock position to attack. The first jet barely cleared the B-26 flown by the flight leader, Lieutenant Hansen, and the second 262 had to haul back on his stick to avoid it as well. The third enemy fighter barely cleared the

No. 4 aircraft in the bomber formation and looked as if it would ram the rear of Hansen's B-26.

The Luftwaffe pilot dumped his stick and managed to get under Hansen's right engine, but clipped off about half his rudder and vertical stabilizer on the propeller. The 262 moved to the right, which placed it in front of Vining's fixed gun package located in the nose of the Marauder. Vining pressed the trigger and continued to fire until he realized he was pulling out of formation. Vining's B-26 was hit in the rear by a fourth Me 262 that knocked out his right engine, shattered the cockpit and blew off Vining's right foot.

The Sanders' aircraft was seen to continue down and enter the clouds. Two other B-26s in the formation had suffered battle damage, while the Marauder flown by Lieutenant Harvey D. Adams was hit in both engines. With the right engine on fire and the left engine feathered, Adams managed to struggle to friendly territory where he and his crew bailed out.

Meanwhile, Vining was down at 3,000 feet where Technical Sergeant N.C. Armstrong managed to put a tourniquet on his leg. Vining told his copilot, Lieutenant Jim Mulvihill, to begin seeking a place to put the aircraft down while he flew the plane so the bombardier, Staff Sergeant J.D. Wells, could get out of the nose. This maneuver required Mulvihill to slide his seat back so Wells could get out. This barely accomplished, Vining passed out.

The crash landing would probably have been successful had they not hit an unobserved tank trap that caused the aircraft to break up, killing the top turret gunner, Staff Sergeant Bill Winger, and critically injuring Wells. Fortunately, the crash took place beside a hospital train, whose personnel were able to give Vining and Wells immediate treatment. Both of the men survived. Vining was later awarded the Silver Star and Mulvihill the Distinguished Flying Cross for their performances that day.

Hansen and the other damaged Marauder pilots successfully flew their aircraft back to base. The cost to the 323rd was three B-26s, with several others badly damaged, while its men were credited with downing two of the Me 262s.

No further victories were scored against the Luftwaffe jets by Americans until April 24, when the 365th Fighter Group, of the Ninth Air Force, was assigned to escort B-26s attacking oil storage depots at Schrobenhausen, Germany. Major James E. Hill led his 388th Fighter Squadron on the mission.

At 1525 hours, the last of the B-26s were beginning their bomb runs, when four Me 262s broke out of the clouds in line-abreast formation. The 388th Fighter Squadron was flying with Blue and Green Flights, which were led by Captain Jerry G. Mast and Lieutenant Oliven T. Cowan.

They flew up high while Hill with Red Flight and White Flight were down low. Someone in White Flight called in the jets, and Cowan dove down on them from 17,000 feet. He fired two short bursts, observing strikes, but could not stay with the jets due to their high rate of speed. However, he successfully broke up their attack on the bombers.

Mast was 2,000 feet above the B-26s, and he noticed one of the Me 262s that had been scattered after Cowan's pass was coming back in at six o'clock to the bombers. He immediately split-essed and went down after the enemy aircraft, which apparently sighted him, broke off its attack and went into a steep dive to escape.

Lieutenant William N. Myers, in Hill's flight, saw the Me 262 and called it out to Hill, who went into a sharp bank to the left. When someone called out, "I lost him," Myers went straight down after the 262, which was diving away from Mast.

The jet pilot started to pull out, but when he saw two Thunderbolts closing in on him, he steepened his dive. The Me 262 smashed into a small hill at tremendous speed and was completely destroyed.

The P-47 pilots managed to pull out, with Myers blacking out in the process.

Mast and Myers were jointly credited with the destruction of the Me 262, which was later determined to have been flown by renowned Luftwaffe commander and ace, Oberst Gunther Lutzow of JV 44. Lutzow had become an ace with five victories during the Spanish Civil War, and he had led JG 3 during the Battle of Britain.

He was awarded the Knights Cross in September 1940, added the Oak Leaves to the award in July 1941 and won Oak Leaves with Swords in October 1941 when his victory total reached ninety-two while flying on the Eastern Front. He had 108 victories at the time of his death, including two earned while flying the Me 262.

Years later Myers recalled: "For some reason, he went into a dive, and I practically rolled onto my back trying to cut him off. We continued to go straight down until it became apparent that it was quite possible neither of us would be able to pull out of the dive. I later remembered that I had even fired my guns in the early moments, but it was a ridiculous effort since I was much too far away."

Cowan was credited with damaging one of the Me 262s in his initial attack, and Lieutenant Byron Smith, Jr., who dove down with Mast, was also credited with a 262 damaged when he engaged another jet that he had spied on their way down.

Unfortunately, the bombers did not get out of the fight unscathed. Two of the Marauders from the 17th Bomb Group's 34th Bomb Squadron were downed by jets. Aircraft flown by Lieutenants Fred Harms, Jr., and Leigh Slates went down and only the top turret gunner of Harms' crew survived.

APRIL 25, 1945

April 25 proved to be a busy combat day for the jets. The veteran 4th Fighter Group of the Eighth Air Force was out early to attack the airfield at Prague/Ruzyne. Lieutenant William B. Hoelscher caught an Me 262 just after takeoff, latched onto its tail and sprayed it with .50-caliber fire. However, he was hit by flak during his attack and had to break off the chase. He reported seeing the jet crash, as did his wingman. For some strange reason, the claim went into the books as probably destroyed.

Shortly thereafter, Lieutenant Hilton O. Thompson, of the 479th Fighter Group, who had shot down an Me 262 on April 7, came upon and destroyed an Arado 234. He was on an escort mission to Traunstein, Germany, when he spotted a bogie just above him while flying at 24,000 feet. He and his wingman climbed up to identify the craft, and Thompson identified it as an Arado 234.

As the jet turned to the southeast, the Mustang pilot turned in behind it and opened fire from 800 yards. Hits were scored on the left engine, and as the 234 slowed, Thompson closed right in on it. Additional bursts of gunfire blew hunks off the enemy craft, which began to spiral to the right. The pilot bailed out somewhere below 10,000 feet. Thompson's victory marked the last confirmed victory over a German jet by an Eighth Air Force pilot.

The jets went after a formation of B-26s that had attacked German ordnance installations at Erding, but they were intercepted by Mustangs from the 370th Fighter Group, of the Ninth Air Force. The eight or nine Me 262s involved were driven off by the P-51s, and

Oberstleutnant Heinz Bar led 3/EJG 2 while it was training Me 262 pilots, and he downed nine Allied aircraft during that period. Bar claimed another seven American aircraft after he replaced Adolf Galland as leader of JV 44. He finished the war with 220 victories.

Lieutenants Richard D. Stevenson and Robert W. Hoyle shared in the destruction of one of the enemy aircraft. Three other jets were damaged in the encounter.

Eighth Air Force bombers flew their last mission of World War II on this day, and six B-17s were lost to flak. No enemy fighter encounters were reported.

APRIL 26, 1945

On the morning of April 26, General Galland took off at 1100 hours leading a flight of six Me 262s from JV 44's base at Munchen/Riem. One of the jets was forced to abort the mission with engine trouble, while the remaining aircraft headed out to intercept a formation of B-26 Marauders on their way to bomb Schrobenhausen.

About 1200 hours, Galland sighted the formation of Marauders and led his birds in for the attack. He and his wingman went in after a B-26 flying on the outside rear of one vee. In the excitement, Galland failed to release the safety for his rockets, and when they failed to fire, he opened up with the 30 MM guns in the nose. The Marauder exploded in mid-air. Swiftly, Galland lined up on a second B-26 and damaged it heavily before he pulled off to the left of the formation.

Galland came under attack from a P-47 flown by Lieutenant James J. Finnegan of the 1st Tactical Air Force's 50th Fighter Group. Finnegan recalled: "I saw two Me 262s come out of nowhere and in the flick of an eye, literally blew up two bombers. After a moment, I saw one of the 262s below me flying in the opposite direction. I turned over on my back, pulled tight on the stick and almost immediately had the enemy aircraft in my sights.

"I got off two quick bursts but couldn't see if I had hit anything because the nose of my aircraft was pulled too high to get a good lead. However, I dropped the nose and observed what I thought were bits and pieces coming from the cowling. In addition, I saw smoke trailing from the wing.

"I attempted to close in again for another shot, but the German aircraft disappeared into the clouds. Because I never saw it hit the ground, I claimed a damaged in the engagement."

Galland recalled: "A hail of fire enveloped me. A sharp rap hit my right knee. The instrument panel was shattered. The right engine was also hit. Its metal covering worked loose in the wind and was partly carried away. Now the left engine was hit, too. I could hardly hold her in the air."

It took a frantic struggle, but Galland finally coaxed his aircraft back to its airfield, where he found it under attack once again. Aware that he had no choice but to get the plane down, Galland cut his fuel switches and managed to sneak in over the treetops and belly in. Immediately, he pulled himself from the aircraft and was rescued by a mechanic, who came out after him in an armored tractor.

It was not until 1979 that dedicated American historian Henry Sakaida finally solved the mystery of who had downed the famed Luftwaffe General. Finnegan and Galland were formally reunited at San Francisco International Airport on August 21, 1979.

A second Me 262 from JV 44 was downed during the combat. Captain Robert W. Clark successfully destroyed one of the attacking jets, but not before three of the B-26s had been lost. A fourth Marauder from the 17th Bomb Group managed to crash land in friendly territory.

On this same morning, Thunderbolts of the 27th Fighter Group were out on armed reconnaissance missions west of Munich. Several targets of opportunity were sighted and strafed. While diving on a ground target, Captain Herbert A. Philo and his wingman saw an Me 262 pass in front of them, flying right down on the deck.

The two P-47s immediately gave chase, and Philo sent the jet down in flames. This marked the last confirmed victory of an American fighter pilot against a German jet aircraft.

Leadership of JV 44 was taken over by Oberstleutnant Heinz Bar. There were further combats involving the elite unit, but most of the missions seem to have been against Russian opponents.

Combat operations of JG 7 also continued, but they were mostly restricted to ground support operations against Russian forces closing in on Berlin.

WINDING DOWN

An encounter with an Me 262 took place on April 29, when Thunderbolts of the 358th Fighter Group engaged an Me 262. Captain James H. Hall and Lieutenant Joseph Richlitsky were credited with damaging a jet while on a fighter sweep. It is quite possible that their victim was Leutenant Franz Kelb of 1/JG 7, who was killed when his aircraft crashed about this time.

The final jet encounter took place on May 3, when Lieutenants Arnold G. Sarrow and Albert T. Kalvaitis of the 365th Fighter Group damaged an Me 262 during a chase over Prague.

In the months that the German jets had been active, they had presented a definite menace to American bombing operations. While greatly outclassed in speed, American escort fighters had accepted the challenge and had been quite successful in diminishing the threat to the bombers. However, for the Luftwaffe, its failure to menace had plainly been a case of too little, too late.

CONFIRMED JET VICTORIES

EIGHTH AIR FORCE

Date	Rank and Name	Group	Type
7/29/44	Captain Arthur F. Jeffrey	479	Me 163
8/16/44	Lieutenant Colonel John B. Murphy	359	Me 163
8/16/44	Lieutenant Cyril W. Jones, Jr.	359	Me 163
8/28/44	Major Joseph Myers	78	½ Me 262
8/28/44	Lieutenant Manford O. Croy, Jr.	78	½ Me 262
10/7/44	Lieutenant Urban L. Drew	361	2 Me 262
10/7/44	Lieutenant Elmer A. Taylor	364	½ Me 262
10/7/44	Lieutenant Willard G. Erfkap	364	½ Me 262
10/7/44	Major Richard E. Conner	78	Me 262
10/15/44	Lieutenant Huie H. Lamb	78	Me 262
11/1/44	Lieutenant Walter R. Groce	56	½ Me 262
11/1/44	Lieutenant William T. Gerbe, Jr.	352	½ Me 262
11/2/44	Captain Fred W. Glover	4	Me 163
11/2/44	Captain Louis H. Norley	4	Me 163
11/6/44	Lieutenant William J. Quinn	361	Me 262
11/6/44	Captain Charles E. Yeager	357	Me 262
11/8/44	Lieutenant Richard W. Stevens	364	Me 262

GERMAN JETS VS. THE U.S. ARMY AIR FORCE

Date	Rank and Name	Group	Type
11/8/44	Lieutenant Anthony Maurice	361	Me 262
11/8/44	Lieutenant Edward R. Haydon	357	½ Me 262
11/8/44	Captain Ernest C. Fiebelkorn	20	½ Me 262
11/8/44	Lieutenant James W. Kenney	357	Me 262
11/18/44	Lieutenant John M. Creamer	4	½ Me 262
11/18/44	Captain John C. Fitch	4	½ Me 262
12/9/44	Lieutenant Harry L. Edwards	352	Me 262
12/31/44	Lieutenant Colonel John C. Meyer	352	Ar 234
1/1/45	Lieutenant Franklin W. Young	4	Me 262
1/13/45	Lieutenant Walter J. Konantz	55	Me 262
1/14/45	Lieutenant Billy J. Murray	353	Me 262
1/14/45	Lieutenant John W. Rohrs	353	½ Me 262
1/14/45	Lieutenant George J. Rosen	353	½ Me 262
1/15/45	Lieutenant Robert P. Winks	357	Me 262
1/20/45	Lieutenant Roland R. Wright	357	Me 262
1/20/45	Lieutenant Dale E. Karger	357	Me 262
2/9/45	Captain Donald H. Bochkay	357	Me 262
2/9/45	Lieutenant Johnnie L. Carter	357	Me 262
2/9/45	Lieutenant Stephen C. Ananian	339	Me 262
2/15/45	Lieutenant Dudley M. Amoss	55	Me 262

CONFIRMED JET VICTORIES

Date	Rank and Name	Group	Type
2/21/45	Lieutenant Harold E. Whitmore	356	Me 262
2/22/45	Major Wayne K. Blickenstaff	353	Me 262
2/22/45	Captain Gordon B. Compton	353	Me 262
2/22/45	Lieutenant Charles D. Price	352	Me 262
2/25/45	Lieutenant Carl G. Payne	4	Me 262
2/25/45	Captain Donald M. Cummings	55	2 Me 262
2/25/45	Captain Donald E. Penn	55	Me 262
2/25/45	Lieutenant Donald T. Menegay	55	Me 262
2/25/45	Lieutenant Millard O. Anderson	55	Me 262
2/25/45	Lieutenant John F. O'Neil	55	Me 262
2/25/45	Lieutenant Billy Clemmons	55	Me 262
2/25/45	Lieutenant Eugene Murphy	364	½ Ar 234
2/25/45	Lieutenant Richard E. White	364	½ Ar 234
3/1/45	Lieutenant Wendell W. Beaty	355	Me 262
3/1/45	Lieutenant John K. Wilkins	2AD Scout	Me 262
3/14/45	Lieutenant Robert E. Barnhart	356	Ar 234
3/14/45	Lieutenant Sanborn N. Ball, Jr.	56	½ Ar 234
3/14/45	Lieutenant Warren S. Lear	56	½ Ar 234
3/14/45	Lieutenant Norman D. Gould	56	Ar 234
3/14/45	Captain Donald S. Bryan	352	Ar 234

Date	Rank and Name	Group	Type
3/15/45	Captain Ray S. Wetmore	359	Me 163
3/19/45	Major Niven K. Cranfill	359	Me 262
3/19/45	Major Robert W. Foy	357	Me 262
3/19/45	Captain Robert S. Fifield	357	Me 262
3/19/45	Lieutenant Huie H. Lamb	78	½ Ar 234
3/19/45	Captain Winfield H. Brown	78	½ Ar 234
3/19/45	Lieutenant James E. Parker	78	Ar 234
3/19/45	Captain Charles H. Spencer	355	Me 262
3/20/45	Lieutenant Robert E. Irion	339	Me 262
3/20/45	Lieutenant Vernon N. Barto	339	Me 262
3/21/45	Lieutenant Harry M. Chapman	361	Me 262
3/21/45	Lieutenant Niles C. Greer	339	½ Me 262
3/21/45	Lieutenant Billy E. Langohr	339	½ Me 262
3/21/45	Lieutenant Walter E. Bourque	78	Me 262
3/21/45	Lieutenant John A. Kirk	78	Me 262
3/21/45	Captain Edwin H. Miller	78	Me 262
3/21/45	Lieutenant Robert H. Anderson	78	Me 262
3/21/45	Captain Winfield H. Brown	78	½ Me 262
3/21/45	Lieutenant Allen A. Rosenblum	78	½ Me 262
3/22/45	Lieutenant John W. Cunnick	55	Me 262

CONFIRMED JET VICTORIES

Date	Rank and Name	Group	Type
3/22/45	Captain Harold T. Barnaby	78	Me 262
3/22/45	Lieutenant Milton B. Stutzman	78	½ Me 262
3/22/45	Lieutenant Eugene L. Peel	78	½ Me 262
3/25/45	Lieutenant Eugene H. Wendt	479	Me 262
3/25/45	Lieutenant Raymond H. Littge	352	Me 262
3/25/45	Lieutenant Edwin H. Crosthwait, Jr.	56	Me 262
3/25/45	Captain George E. Bostwick	56	Me 262
3/30/45	Lieutenant John B. Guy	364	½ Me 262
3/30/45	Unknown P-51 pilot	--	½ Me 262
3/30/45	Lieutenant Thomas V. Thain, Jr.	78	½ Me 262
3/30/45	Lieutenant Colonel John D. Landers	78	½ Me 262
3/30/45	Lieutenant Carroll W. Bennett	339	Me 262
3/30/45	Lieutenant James C. Hurley	352	Me 262
3/30/45	Lieutenant Kenneth J. Scott, Jr.	361	Me 262
3/30/45	Lieutenant Patrick L. Moore	55	Me 262
3/30/45	Captain Robert F. Sargent	339	Me 262
3/31/45	Lieutenant Marvin L. Castleberry	2 AD Scout	Me 262
3/31/45	Lieutenant Wayne L. Coleman	78	Me 262
3/31/45	Lieutenant Harrison B. Tordoff	353	Me 262
4/4/45	Lieutenant Colonel George F. Ceuleers	364	Me 262

GERMAN JETS VS. THE U.S. ARMY AIR FORCE

Date	Rank and Name	Group	Type
4/4/45	Captain Harry R. Corey	339	Me 262
4/4/45	Captain Kirke B. Everson	339	½ Me 262
4/4/45	Lieutenant Robert C. Croker	339	½ Me 262
4/4/45	Lieutenant Nile C. Greer	339	Me 262
4/4/45	Lieutenant Robert C. Havinghurst	339	Me 262
4/4/45	Lieutenant Elmer H. Ruffle	355	Ar 234
4/4/45	Lieutenant Raymond A. Dyer	4	Me 262
4/4/45	Lieutenant Harold H. Frederick	4	½ Me 262
4/4/45	Lieutenant Michael J. Kennedy	4	½ Me 262
4/5/45	Captain John C. Fahringer	56	Me 262
4/7/45	Lieutenant Hilton O. Thompson	479	Me 262
4/7/45	Captain Verne E. Hooker	479	Me 262
4/9/45	Major Edward B. Giller	55	Me 262
4/9/45	Lieutenant James T. Sloan	361	Me 262
4/10/45	Lieutenant Wayne C. Gatlin	356	Me 262
4/10/45	Captain John K. Brown	20	Me 262
4/10/45	Captain Douglas J. Pick	364	Me 262
4/10/45	Captain John K. Hollins	20	Me 262
4/10/45	Lieutenant Albert B. North	20	Me 262
4/10/45	Lieutenant Walter T. Drozd	20	Me 262

CONFIRMED JET VICTORIES

Date	Rank and Name	Group	Type
4/10/45	Flight Officer Jerome Rosenblum	20	½ Me 262
4/10/45	Lieutenant John W. Cudd, Jr.	20	½ Me 262
4/10/45	Lieutenant Jack W. Clark	353	½ Me 262
4/10/45	Lieutenant Bruce D. Memahan	353	½ Me 262
4/10/45	Captain Gordon B. Compton	353	Me 262
4/10/45	Captain Robert L. Abernathy	353	Me 262
4/10/45	Lieutenant Wilmer W. Collins	4	Me 262
4/10/45	Lieutenant Walter J. Sharbo	56	Me 262
4/10/45	Lieutenant Harold Tenenbaum	359	Me 262
4/10/45	Lieutenant Robert J. Guggenos	359	Me 262
4/10/45	Lieutenant Colonel Earl D. Duncan	352	½ Me 262
4/10/45	Major Richard G. McAuliffe	352	½ Me 262
4/10/45	Lieutenant Charles C. Pattilo	352	Me 262
4/10/45	Lieutenant Carlo A. Ricci	352	½ Me 262
4/10/45	Lieutenant Joseph W. Prichard	352	½ Me 262
4/10/45	Lieutenant Keith R. McGinnis	55	Me 262
4/10/45	Lieutenant Kenneth A. Lashbrook	55	Me 262
4/16/45	Major Eugene E. Ryan	55	Me 262
4/17/45	Lieutenant John C. Campbell, Jr.	339	Me 262
4/17/45	Captain Roy W. Orndorff	364	Me 262

Date	Rank and Name	Group	Type
4/17/45	Lieutenant William F. Kissel	364	Me 262
4/17/45	Captain Walter L. Goff	364	Me 262
4/17/45	Flight Officer James A. Steiger	357	Me 262
4/18/45	Lieutenant Colonel Dale E. Shafer, Jr.	339	Ar 234
4/18/45	Lieutenant Leon Oliver	356	Ar 234
4/18/45	Captain Charles E. Weaver	357	Me 262
4/18/45	Major Donald H. Bochkay	357	Me 262
4/19/45	Lieutenant Robert DeLoach	55	Me 262
4/19/45	Lieutenant Paul N. Bowles	357	Me 262
4/19/45	Captain Robert S. Fifield	357	Me 262
4/19/45	Lieutenant Carroll W. Ofsthun	357	Me 262
4/19/45	Lieutenant Gilman L. Weber	357	½ Me 262
4/19/45	Captain Ivan L. McGuire	357	½ Me 262
4/19/45	Lieutenant James P. McMullen	357	Me 262
4/19/45	Lieutenant Colonel Jack W. Hayes, Jr.	357	Me 262
4/25/45	Lieutenant Hilton O. Thompson	479	Ar 234

NINTH AIR FORCE

2/22/45	Lieutenant Oliver T. Cowan	365	Me 262
2/22/45	Lieutenant David B. Fox	366	Me 262

Date	Rank and Name	Group	Type
3/2/45	Lieutenant Theodore W. Sedvert	354	Me 262
3/2/45	Flight Officer Ralph Delgado	354	Me 262
4/14/45	Lieutenant Loyd J. Overfield	354	Me 262
4/14/45	Captain Clayton K. Gross	354	Me 262
4/16/45	Lieutenant Henry A. Yandel	368	Me 262
4/16/45	Lieutenant Vernon D. Fein	368	Me 262
4/17/45	Captain Jack A. Warner	354	Me 262
4/24/45	Captain Jerry G. Mast	365	½ Me 262
4/24/45	Lieutenant William H. Myers	365	½ Me 262
4/25/45	Lieutenant Richard D. Stevenson	370	½ Me 262
4/25/45	Lieutenant Robert W. Hoyle	370	½ Me 262

1ST TACTICAL AIR FORCE

Date	Rank and Name	Group	Type
3/31/45	Captain William T. Bales, Jr.	371	Me 262
4/4/45	Lieutenant Mortimer J. Thompson	324	Ar 234
4/4/45	Lieutenant John W. Haun	324	Me 262
4/4/45	Lieutenant Andrew N. Kandis	324	Me 262
4/8/45	Lieutenant John J. Usiatynski	358	Me 262
4/17/45	Lieutenant James A. Zweizig	371	Me 262

GERMAN JETS VS. THE U.S. ARMY AIR FORCE

Date	Rank and Name	Group	Type
4/26/45	Captain Herbert A. Philo	27	Me 262
4/26/45	Captain Robert W. Clark	50	Me 262

FIFTEENTH AIR FORCE

Date	Rank and Name	Group	Type
12/22/44	Lieutenant Eugene P. McGlauflin	31	½ Me 262
12/22/44	Lieutenant Roy L. Scales	31	½ Me 262
3/22/45	Captain William J. Dillard	31	Me 262
3/24/45	Colonel William A. Daniel	31	Me 262
3/24/45	Lieutenant William M. Wilder	31	Me 262
3/24/45	Captain Kenneth T. Smith	31	Me 262
3/24/45	Lieutenant Raymond D. Leonard	31	Me 262
3/24/45	Lieutenant Forrest M. Keene, Jr.	31	Me 262

FIFTEENTH AIR FORCE

Date	Rank and Name	Group	Type
3/24/45	Lieutenant Roscoe C. Brown	332	Me 262
3/24/45	Flight Officer Charles V. Brantley	332	Me 262
3/24/45	Lieutenant Earl R. Lane	332	Me 262
4/11/45	Lieutenant Benjamin I. Hall III	52	Ar 234
4/18/45	Major Ralph F. Johnson	325	Me 262

CONFIRMED JET VICTORIES

TOP JET DESTROYERS

Fighter Group	Score
357th Fighter Group	18 ½
55th Fighter Group	16
78th Fighter Group	14
339th Fighter Group	12
352nd Fighter Group	9 ½
364th Fighter Group	9

ACKNOWLEDGEMENTS

RECOGNIZING MY "WINGMEN"

I would like to cite two excellent books that contained much vital information on Luftwaffe jet operations and made it possible to match up so many of the combatants in this book. First, I would like to acknowledge *JG 7: The World's First Jet Unit 1944/45* by Manfred Boehme. His operations history and German claims were essential to the overall picture. Secondly, I would like to acknowledge *The Messerschmitt 262 Combat Diary* by John Foreman and S.E. Harvey. Their overall coverage of all the Me 262 combats were a great help. I would also like to thank them for their theory concerning the death of Walter Nowotny, to which I heartily subscribe, and I feel that through their beliefs I have found and substantiated the victory by Richard Stevens.

I would like to thank Mr. Stevens for his kind cooperation and memories of his combat with the Me 262 on November 8, 1944. Strangely, Stevens had no idea whom he had shot down, nor had he ever heard of Walter Nowotny!

A number of pilots with whom I am personally acquainted have described some of their activities and combats with me over the years, and I would like to particularly recognize Ben Drew, Gordon Compton, Art Jeffries, Dale Karger, Clayton Gross and Bill Daniels for their input. The late John Landers and Don Bochkay were also most helpful with their memories. My old Luftwaffe friend, Franz Stigler, has always assisted with his knowledge of flying the Me 262 and of his days with JV 44.

When it comes to photos, I always have an old friend I can turn to, Jeff Ethell. My continued gratitude for his everlasting kind assistance. Also, Mr. Richard Stevens contributed personal photos to the project, while other photos came from the personal collections of Clayton Gross, Ben Drew, Merle Olmsted and O'bie O'Brien. My sincere thanks and appreciation to all.

Further titles featuring the Luftwaffe

LUFTWAFFE SECRET PROJECTS
Fighters 1939-45

Walter Schick & Ingolf Meyer

95 full colour artwork views,
166 line illustrations and 62 b/w
and colour photographs
c176 pages, hardback
282 x 213 mm
1 85780 052 4
due Autumn 1996
US $44.95 / UK £29.95

Germany's incredible fighter projects of 1939-45 are revealed – in detail, showing the technical dominance that their designers could have achieved – shapes and concepts that do not look out of place in the 1990s.

With access to much previously unpublished information, the authors bring to life futuristic shapes that might have terrorised the Allies had the war gone beyond 1945. Full colour action illustrations in contemporary unit markings show vividly what might have been achieved. Careful comparison with later Allied and Soviet aircraft show the legacy handed on, right up to today's stealth aircraft.

This book, which includes much more material than appeared in the initial German language edition, makes a fascinating complement to Midland's very successful title *War Prizes* – detailed below.

WAR PRIZES
An illustrated survey of German, Italian and Japanese aircraft brought to Allied countries during and after the Second World War

Phil Butler
Foreword: Capt E.M. 'Winkle' Brown, RN

16 contemporary colour
and 466 b/w photographs
320 pages, hardback
282 x 213 mm
0 904597 86 5
US $49.95 / UK £29.95

Meticulously researched study of the many German, Italian, and Japanese aircraft taken to Allied countries or flown by the Allies during and after the Second World War. With extensive new information, some long held myths debunked and an unrivalled selection of photographs, many previously unpublished. The coverage includes civilian aircraft and sailplanes as well as military types; post-war production of German designs and details of surviving aircraft in museums.

UK chapters include such units as RAE Farnborough, 1426 (Enemy Aircraft) Flight, and many other squadrons, organisations and manufacturers. The US chapters deal with aircraft flown by the USAAF at Wright Field, Freeman Field, and in Europe by 'Watson's Whizzers', the US Navy-led TAIC at Anacostia, TAIUs in Australia, the Philippines, and many other units in all theaters of war.

These and other Midland Publishing titles are available from Midland in the UK (tel 01455 233 747) and Specialty Press in the USA (tel 612-583-3239)